SpringerBriefs in Criminology

International and Comparative Criminology

Series Editor

Ernesto U. Savona, Trento, Italy

For further volumes:
http://www.springer.com/series/11921

Susan Donkin

Preventing Terrorism and Controlling Risk

A Comparative Analysis of Control Orders in the UK and Australia

Springer

Susan Donkin
School of Criminology and Criminal Justice
Griffith University
Mount Gravatt, QLD
Australia

ISSN 2192-8533 ISSN 2192-8541 (electronic)
ISBN 978-1-4614-8704-3 ISBN 978-1-4614-8705-0 (eBook)
DOI 10.1007/978-1-4614-8705-0
Springer New York Heidelberg Dordrecht London

Library of Congress Control Number: 2013946890

Printed on acid-free paper

Springer is part of Springer Science+Business Media (www.springer.com)

To my family, near and far

Acknowledgments

This Brief is largely based on my doctoral thesis, which examined the evolution of pre-emption in anti-terrorism law. Having previously undertaken research in the field of crime science, the numerous parallels that exist between mechanisms of crime prevention and terrorism control orders became increasingly evident throughout my candidature.

In acknowledging those who have helped in the development of both this Brief and the ideas presented within it, I would like to begin by expressing my gratitude to former supervisors and now colleagues, Associate Prof. Janet Ransley and Prof. Mark Finnane for their continued mentorship and guidance. Moreover, I extend thanks to Prof. Ernesto Savona, Dr. Benoit Leclerc, Prof. Sheldon Zhang and Prof. Simon Bronitt for their insightful comments on earlier versions of this document. Furthermore, I am grateful to the School of Criminology and Criminal Justice at Griffith University, the Australian Research Council Centre of Excellence in Policing and Security, and in particular, Springer for giving me the opportunity to combine my two passions.

Finally, and most importantly, I thank Dan Birks for his continued patience, support and invaluable feedback finalising this manuscript.

Contents

Figures

Tables

Abstract

The last decade ushered in the introduction of several precautionary control mechanisms transcending preconceived categories of law, procedure and risk to deal with individuals thought to pose a danger to the state or its citizens. Exemplified by control order regimes in the UK and Australia, this precautionary approach to anti-terrorism law has been repeatedly challenged due to the extent of restrictions imposed on individuals suspected of posing a terrorist threat without being found guilty of any offence. When subject to a control order, controlees are required to adhere to restrictions on movement and association, which aim to disrupt opportunities to engage in terrorist activity, and/or increase the risks of detection. In this way, the control order bears distinct similarities with several crime prevention strategies.

The purpose of this Brief is two-fold. The first is to conduct a comparative legal analysis of the control order schemes in the UK and Australia. Thus, in the first half of this Brief, the author examines the implications of having pre-emptive measures incorporated into statute, particularly where it interferes with established legal doctrines. The second objective is to compare the underlying mechanisms of control orders to those used in situational crime prevention (SCP), examining whether pre-emptive laws are in conflict with situational strategies. Synthesising the key points of the opportunity theories and SCP, the parallels between SCP techniques and control order mechanisms are highlighted. The Brief concludes by analysing the rationale and mechanisms behind control order restrictions, and examines them in light of crime prevention theory and practice; suggesting that control order restrictions are, in essence, legislated versions of SCP mechanisms. As such, control orders and similarly precautionary legislation are not in conflict with opportunity reducing strategies, they *are* the strategies reducing the opportunities, relying on increasing risk and effort, removing excuses and reducing provocations.

Keywords Control orders · Terrorism prevention · Situational crime prevention · Anti-terrorism · Pre-emption · Precautionary approach

Chapter 1
The Pre-emptive Turn in Criminal Justice

1.1 Introduction

Over the last decade, several scholars described a change in criminal law procedures (Ashworth 2009; Crawford 2006; Dershowitz 2006; Ericson 2007; Gross 2003; Zedner 2009b), many identifying a shift towards a pre-emption paradigm in the post 9/11 era (De Goede 2008; Lendermann 2009; McCulloch 2009; McCulloch and Carlton 2006; McCulloch and Pickering 2009, 2010; Zedner 2007b, 2009a). A considerable terminology around the legal preventive framework has developed to describe what Dershowitz called "a conceptual shift in emphasis" (2006, p. 2) from deterrence to prevention, signalling an increasing trend away from traditional reactive criminal justice principles (Dyzenhaus and Thwaites 2007; Lynch et al. 2010). For instance, McCulloch (2009) described pre-crime as criminalising "acts that have never happened to deal with threats that are not yet and may never be" (p. 152), its rationale being the prevention of harm via the pre-emption of threats. McCulloch and Pickering described its "anticipatory logic [as] the antithesis of the temporally linear post-crime criminal justice process that commences from the presumption of innocence and progresses through a number of discrete stages involving investigation, collecting evidence, charge, trial and, in the case of a guilty verdict, punishment" (2009, p. 632). Pre-crime and pre-emption thus imply a temporal shift, where reacting to crime becomes secondary to preventing it (Zedner 2007a). However, Zedner (2007b, p. 192) argued that pre-emption differs from prevention: "Whereas the preventive turn of the criminal law is triggered in the main by acts 'more than merely preparatory' to a specified offence, pre-emption legitimates substantial curtailments of individual liberty at earlier points in time—often without the requirement of *mens rea*, still less *actus reus*." Many of the observations and critiques related specifically to departures from criminal law principles and safeguards, and the resultant effect on civil liberties. Frequently associated with terrorism post 9/11, a prominent exemplar of this apparently new pre-emptive trend is the control order scheme introduced in both the United Kingdom and Australia in 2005.

S. Donkin, *Preventing Terrorism and Controlling Risk*, Springer Briefs in International and Comparative Criminology, DOI: 10.1007/978-1-4614-8705-0_1,

Control orders, a preventive order against terrorism suspects for whom there is insufficient evidence to prosecute introduced in Britain[1] and Australia, are a commonly cited example of the new breed of pre-emptive measure. Their application has been highly controversial in both countries (Attorney-General's Department 2008; Security Legislation Review Committee 2006; Zedner 2009a). Several scholars found that legal principles and civil liberties have been put under substantial strain by the new pre-emptive measures (Bronitt 2008; Goldsmith 2008; Keyzer and Blay 2006), compromising some of the fundamental rights we seem to take for granted (Roach 2007). There are several concerns. Control orders can be imposed without any conviction or even evidence of terrorist activity. In this sense, they signal a dramatic departure not only from conventional, reactive criminal law, but also sex offender detention orders, which are triggered after a conviction. Suspects must thus be correctly identified through intelligence if this measure is to be effective (Ruddock 2007). Unlike other offences, the burden of proof required is only *on the balance of probabilities*, i.e. the civil standard of proof. This is because control orders are administratively issued (not as part of the judicial process) civil orders, designed to severely restrict movement, but not deprive individuals of liberty. However, breaching the obligations set out in a control order is punishable by up to five years imprisonment, leading scholars to refer to them as hybrids between civil and criminal law (Ashworth 2009; Bonner 2006). Described as civil preventive orders by the British Home Office, and "specialist executive restraint orders" by Walker (2011, p. 300), critics argue they destabilise the very foundations of our adversarial system of justice, which is built upon the right to a fair trial, the presumption of innocence and transparency of court proceedings (Bonner 2007; Lynch 2006a; Lynch and Williams 2006; McCulloch and Pickering 2009; Zedner 2007b, 2009a), leading some to liken control orders to the restraints of liberty that apply to persons on bail pending trial, or parole post conviction (Walton 2005).

1.2 Old Wine in New Bottles?

The use of preventive orders without conviction is not unique to control orders, nor indeed to the post 9/11 era (Bronitt 2003). For example, in Britain, in addition to the Anti-Social Behaviour Order (ASBO), there is also the Sexual Offences Prevention Order, issued to protect individuals from serious sexual harm. Ashworth and Zedner (2007) argued that public protection was a key driving factor in the introduction and justification for such orders. Moreover, they proposed that even given this rationale, procedural safeguards need to be in place, and that the restrictions imposed should be proportionate to the risk posed. The control order

[1] In Britain, control orders were replaced with Terrorism Prevention and Investigation Measures in late 2011.

regime illustrates the juxtaposition between risk and uncertainty, placing its jurisdiction away from the criminal process, into an administrative realm with increased executive power. Much of this development has been justified in the name of pre-emption (McGarrity and Williams 2010).[2]

In addition to the challenges to traditional legal frameworks the pre-emptive turn in criminal justice also impacts on criminological thoughts and theories. Along with the debate about imposing punishment only after a finding of guilt, notions of risk and its use in the management of individuals and populations have also evolved over the past few decades, culminating in the recent application of the precautionary principle. Sharing many of the same characteristics as pre-emption, the precautionary principle advocates preventative action even in the absence of evidence in cases where the potential consequences of not intervening could be catastrophic, serious and irreversible (Sunstein 2003). Of course, attempting to prevent crime and to protect the public is not novel. The criminal justice system has a long history of preventive legal interventions, such as the habitual criminals legislation in the 19th century, mental health law, and dangerous offender legislation (Finnane and Donkin 2013), not forgetting various preventive policing strategies (Zedner 2006).

Beyond preventive legal interventions, a rich literature on crime prevention has flourished over the past few decades. Crime prevention can take many forms, from environmental design to early identification of offenders and incarceration (Brantingham and Faust 1976). Of particular relevance here, the field of environmental criminology focuses on the criminal event and its proximate causes, suggesting that these are easier to both identify and manipulate than other distal factors (Wortley and Mazerolle 2011). Applying insight from three supportive approaches of environmental criminology, situational crime prevention (SCP) aims to design and implement crime prevention interventions that reduce crime by reducing the opportunities for crime.

Control orders and SCP interventions share a common aim—reducing the potential offender's opportunities to offend. Despite this common goal, the two approaches differ in a number of important ways: firstly, SCP traditionally focuses on the target or environment, whereas the control order focuses on the individual; secondly, SCP interventions do not generally restrict human rights and freedoms, while many of the control order mechanisms exert coercive control over a

[2] Many have argued that the emergence of pre-emption in the criminal justice system is a result of integrating the national security paradigm in reaction to terrorism, as well as influencing anti-terrorism discourse (De Goede 2008; McCulloch 2009; McCulloch and Pickering 2010; Zedner 2007a, 2009b). McCulloch (2009) highlighted the inherent tension between the supposedly impartial criminal justice system and the inherently political national security strategy. Also, national security has much more of a pre-emptive aim than does the criminal justice system. However, rather than being the trigger for this pre-emptive shift, Dershowitz believed that 9/11 simply legitimated it, citing several historical precedents.

particular individual, thus raising important ethical and legal issues. Importantly however, SCP and control orders do share a number of key techniques in controlling opportunities to undertake illegal activity, and as such, these two approaches can inform one another.

1.3 Purpose of Study

The purpose of this study is twofold: (1) to conduct a comparative legal analysis of the control order schemes in the UK and Australia; and (2) to compare the underlying mechanisms of control orders to those used in SCP, examining whether pre-emptive laws are in conflict with situational strategies. Thus, in the first half of this Brief, I examine the implications of incorporating pre-emptive measures into statute, particularly where this interferes with established legal doctrines. In Chap. 2, I begin by examining the key critiques levelled at control orders, focusing on the procedural issues and human rights implications arising from their hybrid nature. Chapter 3 provides a brief statutory analysis of control orders in the United Kingdom and Australia, before presenting a more detailed case analysis examining how control orders have been implemented and challenged in the two countries in Chap. 4. Subsequently, Chap. 5 examines the justification of such control regimes, tracing the evolution of risk and protecting the public from dangerous individuals and groups via the rise of actuarial justice to the precautionary approach. The alleged risk posed by controlees is used to justify the restrictive opportunity reducing strategies imposed on these individuals. Thus, to address the second objective, I synthesise the key points of the opportunity theories and situational crime prevention, highlighting the parallels between SCP interventions and control orders in Chap. 6. The final chapter dissects the rationale and mechanisms behind control order restrictions and examines them in light of crime prevention theory and practice. I propose that not only are control orders not in conflict with opportunity reducing strategies, they *are* the strategies reducing the opportunities. As such, I suggest that pre-emptive measures represent a new type of crime controller, exerting direct coercive and enforceable control over the potential offender, ultimately enabled by the precautionary principle.

References

Ashworth, A. (2009). Criminal law, human rights and preventative justice. In B. McSherry, A. Norrie & S. Bronitt (Eds.), *Regulating deviance: the redirection of criminalisation and the futures of criminal law*. Oxford and Portland OR: Hart Publishing.

Ashworth, A., & Zedner, L. (2007). Defending the criminal law: Reflections on the changing character of crime, procedure, and sanctions. *Criminal Law and Philosophy, 2*(1), 21–51.

Attorney-General's Department. (2008). Annual report 2007–08. Canberra: Commonwealth of Australia.

Bonner, D. (2006). Checking the executive? Detention without trial, control orders, due process and human rights. *European Public Law, 12*(1), 45–71.

Bonner, D. (2007). *Executive measures, terrorism and national security: have the rules of the game changed?* Aldershot: Ashgate.

Brantingham, P. J., & Faust, F. L. (1976). A conceptual model of crime prevention. *Crime & Delinquency, 22*(3), 284–296.

Bronitt, S. (2003). *Australia's legal response to terrorism: Neither novel nor extraordinary?* Paper presented at the Castan Centre For Human Rights Law Conference "Human Rights 2003: The Year in Review", Melbourne.

Bronitt, S. (2008). Balancing security and liberty: critical perspectives on terrorism law reform. In M. Gani & P. Mathew (Eds.), *Fresh perspectives on the war on terror*. Canberra: ANU E Press.

Crawford, A. (2006). Networked governance and the post-regulatory state? Steering, rowing and anchoring the provision of policing and security. *Theoretical Criminology, 10*(4), 449–479.

De Goede, M. (2008). The politics of preemption and the war on terror in Europe. *European Journal of International Relations, 14*(1), 161–185. doi: 10.1177/1354066107087764.

Dershowitz, A. M. (2006). *Preemption: A knife that cuts both ways*. New York: W.W. Norton & Company.

Dyzenhaus, D., & Thwaites, R. (2007). Legality and emergency—The Judiciary in a time of terror. In A. Lynch, E. MacDonald & G. Williams (Eds.), *Law and liberty in the war on terror*. Sydney: The Federation Press.

Ericson, R. V. (2007). *Crime in an insecure world*. Cambridge: Polity Press.

Finnane, M., & Donkin, S. (2013). Fighting terror with law? Some other genealogies of pre-emption. *International Journal for Crime and Justice, 2*(1), 3–17.

Goldsmith, A. (2008). The governance of terror: Precautionary logic and counterterrorist law reform after September 11. *Law & Policy, 30*(2), 141–167.

Gross, O. (2003). Chaos and rules: Should responses to violent crises always be constitutional? *The Yale Law Journal, 112*(5), 1011–1134.

Keyzer, P., & Blay, S. (2006). Double punishment—Preventive detention schemes under Australian Legislation and Their Consistency with International Law: The Fardon Communication Commentary *Melbourne Journal of International Law, 7*(2), 407–424.

Lendermann, M. (2009). Prävention durch Recht–Kann normative auf Terrorismus reagiert werden? (Prevention through law: can one react normatively to terrorism?). *Humbolt Forum Recht* (12), 163–175.

Lynch, A. (2006a). Legislating with urgency—The Enactment of the Anti-Terrorism Act [No 1] 2005. *Melbourne University Law Review 30*(3), 747–781.

Lynch, A., & Williams, G. (2006). *What price security? Taking Stock of Australia's Anti-Terror Laws*. Sydney, NSW: University of New South Wales Press Ltd.

Lynch, A., McGarrity, N., & Williams, G. (2010). The emergence of a 'culture of control'. In N. McGarrity, A. Lynch & G. Williams (Eds.), *Counter-terrorism and beyond: The culture of law and justice after 9/11*. London: Routledge.

McCulloch, J. (2009). *Precrime: Imagining future crime and a new space for criminology*. Paper presented at the Australia and New Zealand Critical Criminology Conference, Melbourne. http://arts.monash.edu.au/criminology/c3-conference-proceedings/anz-critical-criminology-conference-2009-proceedings.pdf.

McCulloch, J., & Carlton, B. (2006). Preempting justice: Suppression of financing of terrorism and the war on terror. *Current Issues in Criminal Justice, 17*, 397.

McCulloch, J., & Pickering, S. (2009). Pre-crime and counter-terrorism: Imagining future crime in the 'War on Terror'. *British Journal of Criminology, 49*, 628–645.

McCulloch, J., & Pickering, S. (2010). Counter-terrorism: The law and policing of pre-emption. In N. McGarrity, A. Lynch & G. Williams (Eds.), *Counter-terrorism and beyond: The culture of law and justice after 9/11*. London: Routledge.

McGarrity, N., & Williams, G. (2010). When extraordinary measures become normal: Pre-emption in counter-terrorism and other laws. In N. McGarrity, A. Lynch & G. Williams

(Eds.), *Counter-terrorism and beyond: The Culture of law and justice after 9/11*. London: Routledge.

Roach, K. (2007). The case for defining terrorism with restraint and without reference to political or religious motive. In A. Lynch, E. MacDonald & G. Williams (Eds.), *Law and liberty in the war on terror*. Sydney: Federation Press.

Ruddock, P. (2007). Law as a preventative weapon against terrorism. In A. Lynch, E. MacDonald & G. Williams (Eds.), *Law and liberty in the war on terror*. Sydney: Federation Press.

Security Legislation Review Committee. (2006). Report of the Security Legislation Review Committee. Canberra: Commonwealth of Australia.

Sunstein, C. R. (2003). Beyond the precautionary principle. *University of Pennsylvania Law Review, 151*(3), 1003–1058.

Walker, C. (2011). *Terrorism and the law*. Oxford: Oxford University Press.

Walton, M. (2005). The anti-terrorism bill (No. 2) 2005: An overview. *Human Rights Defender, 9* (Special Issue).

Wortley, R., & Mazerolle, L. (2011). Environmental criminology and crime analysis: situating the theory, analytic approach and application. In R. Wortley & L. Mazerolle (Eds.), *Environmental criminology and crime analysis*. Abingdon: Routledge.

Zedner, L. (2006b). Policing before and after the police. *British Journal of Criminology, 46*(1), 78–96. doi: 10.1093/bjc/azi043.

Zedner, L. (2007a). Pre-crime and post-criminology. *Theoretical Criminology, 11*, 261–281.

Zedner, L. (2007). Preventive justice or pre-punishment? The case of control orders. *Current Legal Problems, 60*(1), 174–203. doi: 10.1093/clp/60.1.174.

Zedner, L. (2009a). Fixing the future? The Pre-emptive turn in criminal justice. In B. McSherry, A. Norrie & S. Bronitt (Eds.), *Regulating deviance: the redirection of criminalisation and the futures of criminal law*. Oxford and Portland OR: Hart Publishing.

Zedner, L. (2009b). *Security*. Abingdon: Routledge.

Chapter 2
Preventing Terrorism: An Exceptional Legal Hybrid?

2.1 Introduction

Since their introduction in 2005, terrorism control orders have been divisive owing to their ability to impose serious restrictions and obligations on individuals' liberty based on an intelligence-led, low standard of proof in a civil process originating with the Executive. Advocates of the scheme, of whom there are comparatively few, argued that control orders were performing an important function, albeit imperfectly (Simcox 2010). While some acknowledged that such impositions on individual liberty without prior conviction may be seen as controversial, they believed the enormous threat to public safety posed by terrorism is sufficient justification (Ruddock 2007). On the other hand, control orders have been widely criticised by politicians, civil liberties organisations and academics alike, much of the criticism focusing on procedural issues and human rights implications. Control orders have been described as unsafe, unfair, and undermining the right to a fair trial and the presumption of innocence (Liberty; Zedner 2007), which goes against British traditions of liberty and justice (Bronitt 2008; Bronitt and McSherry 2010). A vocal critic of the scheme, Zedner (2007) described them as "unprecedentedly intrusive" (p. 176). Baroness Kennedy went even further, describing control orders as "absolutely abhorrent and totally disgraceful in its abuse of civil liberties".[1]

Much of the civil liberties criticism of control orders thus relates to this apparent derogation from well-established criminal law safeguards. Yet it is important to highlight that technically, control orders are a civil administrative measure and thus not subject to the same procedural safeguards applied to a criminal trial. Many of these issues have arisen due to the hybrid nature of control orders (McCulloch and Pickering 2010). Much like the Anti-Social Behaviour Order (ASBO)[2] in the UK, the control order is a civil measure designed to prevent the individual from engaging in the type of behaviour giving rise to the order in the first place. However, a breach of any of the conditions set out in the order without

[1] H.L. Debs., Vol. 670, cols 195–196 (1 March 2005).

[2] ASBOs are civil preventive orders designed to protect individuals or neighbourhoods from anti-social behavior and are further discussed in Sect. 2.4.

S. Donkin, *Preventing Terrorism and Controlling Risk*, Springer Briefs in International and Comparative Criminology, DOI: 10.1007/978-1-4614-8705-0_2,

reasonable excuse has the potential to elevate the measure to the criminal realm, and the controlee could face up to 5 years imprisonment. So while the initial conduct may not have brought about prosecution under the traditional criminal justice paradigm, breaching a condition of the order may. In addition to the civil and criminal overlap, control orders have also been described as executive-judicial hybrids (Bonner 2007); while they originate with the Executive, they also require judicial approval. It is essential to consider their administrative origins in any reflection on pre-emptive principles, as this will affect both their underlying aims, as well as the standards against which they should ultimately be evaluated against. It is to this debate that I now turn.

2.2 Legal Hybrids Framing Control Orders

While the control order process is described in more detail in Chap. 3, a brief overview is necessary here to situate the reader. In Australia, control orders originate with the Australian Federal Police (AFP) who present the Attorney General with a copy of the proposed order for consent, before seeking approval from a Federal Magistrates Court. So although they are applied for by the Executive, they require judicial approval on the balance of probabilities that making the order would substantially assist in preventing a terrorist act, or that the person has either provided training to or received training from a listed terrorist organisation. Moreover, the court needs to be satisfied that the conditions set out in the order are reasonably necessary, appropriate and adapted for the purposes of protecting the public from a terrorist act. Australian courts are able to amend or withdraw certain obligations, and are thus not bound by the conditions set out by the AFP. In the UK, the Home Secretary could issue a non-derogating control order if he or she had reasonable suspicion of the individual's involvement in terrorism or believed it necessary to protect the public from a risk of terrorism. Approval from a High Court judge needed to be sought within 7 days. However, unlike the Australian Judiciary, its British counterpart had to approve the order, unless the Home Secretary's reasoning was obviously flawed. Although this process appears judicial, it blurs the boundaries between the Executive and the Judiciary, due to the limited discretion available to British judges.

2.2.1 Separating the Executive from the Judiciary

Pre-empting terrorism events is increasingly a government priority, and this has given rise to new administrative or executive measures to deal with the problem (International Commission of Jurists 2009). According to the International Commission of Jurists (2009), the conventional evidentiary requirements established within the criminal justice system have partly been displaced by a new framework of administrative, civil and immigration law to combat terrorism. Immigration proceedings, for instance, allow governments more discretion due to their greater flexibility in the provision of legal safeguards compared to criminal proceedings. The same applies in control order hearings, where the degree of judicial oversight is limited by the lower standard of proof required to impose an order (Kavanagh 2010). Control orders are issued by the Executive to prevent a terrorist act by an individual suspected of posing a threat to national security before it occurs (International Commission of Jurists 2009).

As Bonner (2007) acknowledged, some observers have rejected claims that control orders are purely executive since court approval is required to issue them.[3] Accordingly, Bonner prefers to refer to them as hybrid powers, due to the British Judiciary's statutory limitations to refuse such requests.[4] This subtle distinction has raised concerns about the Executive undermining the independence of the Judiciary (Lynch et al. 2010). Under the Separation of Powers doctrine, each branch of government maintains a degree of independence from each other. The intrusion of executive power into the judicial role is of particular concern to the doctrine of judicial independence, a bedrock of the rule of law. This aims to ensure that the Judiciary is free from political agendas when deciding on matters of constitution or legal questions. Traditionally, the Judiciary monitors the Executive, ensuring its actions are carried out within the confines of the law.[5] However, Ericson (2007) highlighted that allocating discretion to the administrative branch of government can be beneficial, as it is better equipped to deal with uncertainty and exigency. Conversely, others argue that increasing executive power and discretion to law enforcement undermines liberal-democratic principles, leading to an abandonment of legal guarantees and protections potentially exposing citizens to arbitrary state power (Ericson 2007; McCulloch and Carlton 2006). Bonner warned that executive measures often "lack the transparency and safeguards of the criminal prosecution approach to which they both provide an alternative and a supplemental means of dealing with threats to national security" (2007, p. 352).

History has shown that when national security measures are legally challenged, the courts typically defer to the Executive (Bonner 2007; Dyzenhaus and Thwaites 2007; Zedner 2005). Bonner (2007) argued that executive measures introduced in reaction to national security inherently deviate from the standards expected in criminal law, starting with the presumption of innocence. There have always been

---

[3] Bonner (2007) defined executive measures as "a product of the empowerment through law of the executive branch of government to take action affecting rights of legal individuals, whether people or corporations, without any need for prior judicial approval of that action" (p. 21). For example, all police-initiated matters are executive functions, including the arrest and charge of an individual prior to judicial review in court. Control orders are often referred to as executive measures because they originate with the Home Secretary in the UK or the Australian Federal Police in Australia.

[4] The Australian control order scheme allows for greater judicial discretion, see Sect. 3.3.

[5] In Australia, federal judicial power can only be exerted by courts listed in s 71 of the Constitution, i.e. the High Court, federal courts and state courts.

limited exceptions to this presumption, principally including pre-trial remand procedures. Those exceptions, however, have been narrowly defined by the courts and subject to review, e.g. by habeas corpus. The United Kingdom has long used executive measures against terrorists, ranging from exclusion and deportation on security grounds to internment in Northern Ireland (Bonner 1992, 2007; Walker 1992, 2004, 2011), as have other nations. In Australia, for example, the Minister for Foreign Affairs has increasingly made use of his power to cancel or refuse to reissue a passport post 9/11 (Harris Rimmer 2010). Criminal law is not always considered suitable to effectively deal with the kinds of demands which arise in the context of national security (Bonner 2007). Walker (2011) has highlighted that compared to a criminal process, executive measures allow for greater executive input, free from judicial independence, allowing the prioritisation of national security over individual fairness. For example, one of the concerns raised with control orders is that the Home Secretary could request an order if he or she reasonably suspected[6] the individual of being involved in terrorism-related activity, which is even lower than the civil standard of proof, i.e. on the balance of probabilities (Zedner 2009a).

While the Executive decides on what measures to implement to protect the public, the role of the Judiciary is to decide whether or not these measures are lawful, a role which is not always very popular with the Executive or indeed the general public (Lynch 2006b). The Judiciary has a long-standing history regarding security-related issues, treating them with respect and esteem (Bonner 2006; Zedner 2007). However, some have argued that the role of the courts is not to support the national security agenda of executive government, nor to pander to public fear in deciding cases (Lynch 2006b). Both Dyzenhaus and Thwaites (2007) and Roach (2002) argued that the Judiciary needs to uphold the rule of law and our deep-seated commitments, even during times of crisis or emergency. However, the responsibility of upholding civil liberties should not fall entirely on judges, since their record during both World Wars has been questionable (Bonner 2007; Spjut 1986; White 2007).

Although detention is not generally determined by the Executive, there are instances, usually related to national security and emergency provisions, which empower it to act in such a way. The basis upon which such detention orders are issued are often vaguely defined threats to national security based on unconfirmed intelligence reports. States have long felt it their responsibility to protect their citizens from dangerous acts or individuals, be it from international foes or internal dissidents or groups; and as such, have introduced various measures tailored to both the circumstances and era (Finnane and Donkin 2013; McSherry 2006). In fact, even in cases not relating to national security individuals may be subject to

---

[6] This threshold has been raised to the civil standard in the UK's replacement to control orders, Terrorism Prevention and Investigation Measures (TPIMs).

administrative detention.[7] Using prevention as the justification to circumvent safeguards might not be novel, but Zedner (2007) argued that safeguarding its citizens does not give a state immunity from the law.

Balancing the Executive's mandate of public protection respect for human rights can be controversial enough operating within a single legal framework, as some of the examples in Sect. 2.4 will highlight. However, the hybrid nature of control orders adds yet another layer of complexity. The next section briefly outlines the civil law framework in which control orders are administered, before contrasting it to the criminal system against which they are frequently measured.

2.2.2 Civil Versus Criminal Realm

Despite the many criticisms in relation to the apparent departure from criminal procedural safeguards, it is important to reiterate that control orders are in fact civil measures. Civil law deals with disputes between people, seeking remedy, not punishment (the State can be a plaintiff or defendant). In the common law systems, civil law is divided into administrative or regulatory law, and private law. That being said, previously clear distinctions between criminal law and administrative law have become blurred more generally, and not just in relation to anti-terrorism (Ashworth 2000; Australian Law Reform Commission 2003; Bronitt and McSherry 2010; Cotterrell 1992; Mazerolle and Ransley 2005). For instance, serious wrongdoings in regulatory and private law are being criminalised,[8] whereas the criminal law has adopted civil procedures and remedies (Ashworth 2000; Ashworth and Zedner 2010; Mazerolle and Ransley 2005). Importantly, the two types of law differ as to their procedural characteristics. The civil standard of proof is *on the balance of probabilities*. Civil courts are able to impose conditions and injunctions on individuals in reaction to a wrong committed by one person against another, but never criminal punishment in the form of incarceration. The latter, technically, is only possible after a finding of guilt in criminal proceedings (Bronitt and McSherry 2010). Notable exceptions include detention under mental health regimes and immigration detention.[9] Increasingly, however, established criminal law safeguards are being circumvented or supplemented by hybrid or quasi-criminal measures, such as ASBOs and control orders. While incarceration is not necessarily considered at the outset, this "parallel system of questionable

[7] For instance, Australia's *Migration Act 1958* (Cth) provides for compulsory, and in some cases, indefinite administrative detention of unlawful non-citizens prior to deportation on the grounds of community protection (Dyzenhaus and Thwaites 2007). Being civil in nature, migration controls avoid being subject to the more stringent criminal law standards set out in international human rights conventions.

[8] See for instance developments in environmental protection or workplace health and safety, as well as examples in family law (Mazerolle and Ransley 2005).

[9] See Article 5 of the ECHR.

justice" as Zedner (2009b, p. 81) called it, despite operating within the civil realm, imposes severe criminal sanctions if orders are breached. ASBOs and control orders exemplify trends toward legal hybridity in that while the measure is civil, it is aimed at preventing future behaviour, but still has the potential to criminalise future behaviour which, if not subject to an ASBO or control order, would not constitute a criminal offence.[10] As such, the behaviour would certainly not be subject to the same severe sanctions as those issued in criminal cases (Ashworth and Zedner 2007; Ramsay 2009).

Criminal law is, for the most part, retrospective and retributive, reacting to offences or transgressions already committed via prosecution, trial and sentencing. Lacey described criminal law as focusing on "the formally established norms according to which individuals or groups are adjudged guilty or innocent" (Lacey 2002, p. 265). In cases where a defendant pleads not guilty, the burden of proof is on the prosecution to prove his/her guilt *beyond a reasonable doubt*. In order to do so, both the *actus reus*[11] and the *mens rea*[12] need to be established beyond reasonable doubt. Exceptions to the rule include self-defence, diminished responsibility or insanity, in which case the burden of proof rests upon the defendant, though he or she is only required to prove their case on the *balance of probabilities*.[13] If found guilty, the defendant is sentenced and punished, which in most industrialised countries means imprisonment (Hudson 2002).

Having examined the legal foundations of the control order framework, in what follows I outline, in relation to the implementation of control orders, the key controversies caught up in the hybrid framework: the reliance on intelligence as opposed to evidence; its adverse impact on the right to a fair trial; and its emphasis on prevention as opposed to punishment.

2.3 Hybrids in Action

As discussed, control orders are legal hybrids in two senses, in that they blur boundaries between executive and judicial functions, as well as between criminal and civil or administrative measures (Bronitt and Donkin 2012). This section discusses three areas where this hybridity causes tension. Evaluating control order

[10] Nuisance behavior, for example.

[11] Physical element, i.e. the act/crime committed (Latin: guilty act).

[12] Fault element, i.e. the state of mind/intent (Latin: guilty mind).

[13] It is worth noting that these presumptions are being broken down even in criminal law. For instance, there are instances where the onus of proof has been reversed, e.g. in cases of mental impairment, as well as offences where no *mens rea* is required (Ashworth 2000; Bronitt and McSherry 2010; Lynch 2006a, b; McSherry 2004). Lynch (2006b) quoted Chief Justice Spigelman in *Lodhi v The Queen* ((2006) 199 FLR 303, 318) as saying that terrorism has created a "unique legislative regime" with regard to criminalising preparatory acts, due to the decision to have criminal responsibility arise at an earlier stage than for the usual conspiracy charge.

procedures against criminal safeguards highlights several procedural shortcomings. In a nutshell, control orders are criticised for their restrictions on liberty, which some argue are punitive in nature, imposed on the basis of intelligence material that is kept secret from the controlee. The reliance on intelligence adversely affects the right of a controlee to a fair trial. Moreover, they are imposed on individuals against whom insufficient evidence to prosecute exists. Consequently, the first point examines the admissibility of intelligence material as evidence, before discussing how non-disclosure affects an individual's right to a fair trial. I conclude this analysis by highlighting why civil libertarian critiques argue control orders should be evaluated against criminal and not civil standards, namely that the severity of the restrictions exceed the preventive realm, constituting a form of punishment, imposed in a process lacking the basic safeguards.

2.3.1 Evidence Versus Intelligence

Control orders can be issued against individuals suspected of involvement in terrorist activities, but who cannot be prosecuted. Several reasons might exist why prosecution of an individual might be impossible, thus necessitating the issuance of a control order (Zedner 2007). For instance, evidence gathered against a suspect may be inadmissible if it is sensitive in nature or risks the safety of the intelligence source (Manningham-Buller 2005; Roach 2010; Zedner 2007). Moreover, as with other preventive measures, the 'evidence' in control order cases is not required to conform to the stringent rules of evidence in criminal proceedings due to the civil nature of the order. However, intelligence material adduced in control order cases is often afforded considerable weight. It is precisely this lack of evidence as the basis of often severe restrictions which is seen as controversial.

In many ways, intelligence and evidence are diametrically opposed. Unlike evidence, which is amenable to challenge in open court, intelligence is not generally disclosed in open court, and lacking any robust challenge entails a greater risk of unreliability (Roach 2010). As both Lynch (2006b) and Roach (2010) have argued, intelligence is concerned with risk assessment of future conduct, whereas evidence and police work on the other hand are more focused on a particular act or crime after it has been committed. Thus, intelligence is more closely linked to prevention and based on suspicion, whereas evidence is reactive and used to prove someone's guilt (Roach 2010).

Of particular importance to this research is the first distinction, namely that intelligence is focused on future events (Roach 2010; Walker 2011). The aim of intelligence is to gather sufficient information to prevent a crime from occurring in the first place, i.e. pre-empting it. In the context of security, the focus on risk highlights a degree of uncertainty, as much of the intelligence gathered is incomplete and unable to provide the complete picture (Manningham-Buller 2005). Indeed, in a famous speech, the former head of MI5, Dame Eliza Manningham-Buller repeatedly pointed out that much of the terrorism-related intelligence post 9/11 was too fragmented and uncertain to even warrant assessment and interpretation, never mind meeting the standards of admissibility required to be adduced as evidence in court (Manningham-Buller 2005; Press Association 2003; Roach 2010). The testing of evidence in cases involving national security is restricted, making meaningful review of decisions challenging (Dyzenhaus and Thwaites 2007). However, Bonner (1992) warned that even good intelligence can still fall short of the standards of evidence.

Some have argued that the advent of preventive measures has increasingly blurred the boundaries between evidence and intelligence (Lynch 2006a, b; Pickering et al. 2008; Ransley and Donkin 2009; Roach 2010; The Street Review 2008). According to the Eminent Jurists Panel, risk has replaced proof (International Commission of Jurists 2009). Imposing restrictions on individuals found on the balance of probabilities to pose a risk to others is not unique to anti-terrorism or control orders, domestic violence and mental health orders being other examples (McDonald 2007; McSherry 2002). In the UK, there have been repeated calls[14] to admit intercept evidence in control order and terrorism cases (Carlile and Berriew 2011; Macdonald 2007), something which Australia has permitted for many decades.[15] In Australia, legislation[16] already enables the use of intelligence in place of evidence in organised crime control orders (Appleby and Williams 2010; Lynch et al. 2010). However, some critics argue that the reliance on intelligence material in such cases raises concerns about the lack of procedural safeguards, which although not technically required in civil cases, should be adhered to given the seriousness of the suspicions against the individual.

2.3.2 Procedural Safeguards

A central tenet of civil libertarian critique of control orders is that they fundamentally undermine the basic and fundamental presumptions of criminal procedures (Ashworth 2006; Bonner 2006; Lynch 2006a; Lynch and Williams 2006; McSherry 2006; Zedner 2007, 2009b). While there is much debate around the universality of criminal law principles (Bronitt and McSherry 2010, p. 86 ff), there are certain protections afforded to defendants in criminal proceedings, so-called procedural safeguards, which are considered a basic and fundamental principle of a fair trial in many countries, although there is considerable variation between

[14] By Lords Lloyd and Newton, as well as the DPP, to name but a few.

[15] *Telecommunications (Interception and Access) Act 1979 (Cth).*

[16] Section 3 of the *Serious and Organised Crime (Control) Act 2008* (SA), which sets out the making of control orders in an organized crime context, defines criminal intelligence as "information relating to actual or suspected criminal activity…the disclosure of which could reasonably be expected to prejudice criminal investigations, to enable the discovery of the existence or identity of a confidential source of information relevant to law enforcement or to endanger a person's life or physical safety".

jurisdictions (Ashworth 2000; Metcalfe 2009). These safeguards typically include the rights to be informed of the accusation against oneself, to be heard,[17] to confront one's accuser, the right to legal counsel, equality of arms,[18] and the presumption of innocence (Metcalfe 2009). Conceived to protect individuals from arbitrary state power and against miscarriages of justice (McCulloch and Carlton 2006), these safeguards have been enshrined in both domestic law and international human rights instruments. However, these conventions or treaties often fulfil more of a symbolic value, as they are not automatically binding on signatory states, and can be derogated from in emergencies.[19] In western democracies, fairness is a fundamental and universal presumption of law, legitimising the criminal justice process (Bronitt and McSherry 2010), making the observance of procedural safeguards all the more important in cases involving serious offences such as terrorism.

Several concerns have been raised in control order cases, many of them related to the absence of the defendant from the process, the closed nature of the proceedings and a process which, as a result, is no longer fully adversarial. Moreover, in the UK, control order hearings are frequently conducted in closed sessions, i.e. behind closed doors, excluding the public and, more importantly, the defendant. In an effort to address some of these critiques, a system of Special Advocates[20] was introduced. Indeed, Baroness Kennedy warned that hearing secret evidence would turn the High Court into a secret commission (Bonner 2006).

The use of closed sessions and Special Advocates severely compromises the right to a fair trial, putting the controlee at a serious disadvantage (Bonner 2006, 2007). Indeed, Kavanagh (2010) expressed doubts over the extent to which a system of Special Advocates is able to deliver a procedurally fair outcome. However, Article 6 of the ECHR (right to a fair hearing) only applies to criminal proceedings,[21] and since control order proceedings are subject to civil rules of evidence, they do not provide individuals with the same safeguards afforded in criminal trials (Ashworth and Zedner 2007, 2010). It has been argued that control

---

[17] To make representation and to challenge any evidence relied upon in court.

[18] Being informed of all the evidence relied upon by the other party or the judge, so as to be able to challenge it in court.

[19] Under Article 15 of the ECHR for example.

[20] Special Advocates have two functions, namely to 'disclose' and 'represent', meaning they are able to view the incriminating, classified material upon which the applicant relies; and to make representations on those materials on their client's behalf (Bonner 2007; Kavanagh 2010). However, once they have been party to the secret material, Special Advocates are prohibited from further communicating with the person they represent. So, if a control order is issued to an individual against whom the court believes material linking him to terrorist-related activities exists, which is not disproved (Bonner 2006), he or she is left with virtually no opportunity to defend him/herself against the accusations. In addition to conflicting with the human rights provisions, a system relying on ex parte hearings, Special Advocates and closed sessions can no longer be considered fully adversarial (Bonner 2006, 2007; Joint Committee on Human Rights 2005; Kavanagh 2010; Metcalfe 2009).

[21] And explicitly excludes immigration hearings.

orders were deliberately set up as a civil preventive executive measure to avoid having to guarantee the individual a fair trial as required under Article 6 of the ECHR, which only applies in criminal proceedings (Joint Committee on Human Rights 2006; Zedner 2007).[22] This view is also shared by Lynch, McGarrity and Williams with regard to the Australian scheme, arguing that the civil nature of the orders make them more "flexible" (Lynch et al. 2010, p. 6). Ashworth and Zedner (2010) described the designation of civil preventive orders as non-criminal a problem of under criminalisation[23] given the failure to comply with criminal procedural safeguards in cases with potentially serious consequences; arguing that criminal proceedings should not be replaced with civil ones in cases that might result in a deprivation of liberty (Ashworth and Zedner 2007).

2.3.3 Restriction Versus Deprivation of Liberty

Traditionally, the deprivation of liberty is seen as a severe punishment for serious offences reserved for use following a guilty verdict in a criminal trial, and often as a last resort (Ashworth 2002; Cohen 1979; von Hirsch 1990). Non-criminal detention is reserved for specific situations, often where there is a risk of harm to a specific individual or the population as a whole, for instance in mental health cases or to prevent the spread of infectious diseases. In those situations detention is justified under the proviso of protection or prevention, not for the purposes of punishment.

The hybrid nature of control orders also affects the issue of deprivation of liberty, particularly in the UK where curfews imposed on controlees were often significantly longer than in Australia. In reality, even under the non-derogating control order the conditions have been described as considerably inhibiting any normal life (Carlile and Berriew 2006), even equating to house arrest (Zedner 2007). It is important to reiterate that civil proceedings are not in a position to assign punishment. Control orders are intended to be preventive in nature, not punitive. That being said, restrictions or even detention appear more legitimate if labelled as preventive, thus sufficiently distinguishing them from punishment (Pratt 1997; Zedner 2009b).

Punishment in the form of a custodial sentence is generally proportionate to the crime and its duration determined at the sentencing stage. Exceptions are made in cases of serious or violent offenders, where protecting the public from serious

[22] Zedner (2007) highlighted that a state's designation of a measure as non-criminal is not always sufficient to avoid it being interpreted as such by the ECHR. The status of control orders as criminal proceedings has been called into question by both the Council of Europe Commissioner for Human Rights and the Joint Human Rights Committee (JHRC) (Bonner 2007).

[23] Contrary to previous research with described an increasing trend towards criminalising behaviour (Ashworth 2000; Crawford 2006).

harm justifies longer periods of detention[24] (Ashworth 2002, 2005; McSherry and Keyzer 2009). There are different aims of criminal sanctions, including deterrence, both specific and general, incapacitation, rehabilitation, retribution, and, perhaps the most overarching and relevant here, the protection of harm to others (Ashworth 2005; Cornall 2007; Ip 2007; Walker 1982). Viewed through the lens of deterrence, punishment, although reactive, also has a clear preventive and future-orientated rationale to it (Bronitt and McSherry 2010). This applies both for the individual who is deterred from offending in the first place, in which case it pre-emptively prevents, and the offender who decides not to re-offend, hence being reactively preventive. That being said, well established doctrines and judgments purport that punishing anticipated future conduct is wrong (Blackstone 1769; Duff and Garland 1994), as it compromises long-established procedural safeguards (Keyzer and Blay 2006; Lynch 2006a). Without a finding of guilt detention is considered arbitrary if its aim is punishment (McSherry 2006; McSherry and Keyzer 2009). However, the dichotomy between what does and does not constitute punishment is fraught with difficulty considering that even if the aim of a preventive measure may not be punishment, the resultant detention will often be perceived and experienced as such (McSherry 2006). This perception is likely heightened if there is no finding of guilt, merely suspicion of involvement. Still, it is important to reiterate at this point that the control orders issued in both the UK and Australia have not amounted to preventive detention requiring derogation.

Nevertheless, critics contend that there are three reasons why control orders can be argued to be punitive in nature (Joint Committee on Human Rights 2006; Zedner 2007). The first reason relates back to the issue of evidence, or rather, the lack thereof in control order cases. For a control order to be issued, there must be a suspicion of involvement in terrorist-related activity, a serious allegation of being guilty of or preparing for a very serious criminal offence. Yet no evidence for such 'charges' is required, as the controlee would arguably only be guilty of such offences at some point in the future. Secondly, despite control orders being civil in nature, the serious restrictions on liberty of even non-derogating orders are more onerous than the traditional civil ones, coming close to being equivalent to criminal punishment in their severity (Zedner 2007). Restrictions on movement and house arrest have been described as a de facto loss of liberty (International Commission of Jurists 2009). Moreover, with the potential of indefinite annual renewal, such restrictions could extend beyond the duration of traditional criminal sanctions (Zedner 2007). Finally, the unintentional breach of one of the obligations by a controlee, something even Lord Carlile highlighted would be quite easy to do (Carlile and Berriew 2006), could result in a prison sentence of up to 5 years.

The potentially punitive character of control orders raises a philosophical debate about the moral justifications of punishing someone prior to committing an

---

[24] In the case of serious sex offenders, for example, where any detention imposed in addition to their completed sentence must be non-punitive in nature to be constitutionally valid (*Fardon v Attorney-General (Qld)* (2004) 223 CLR 575).

offence. Zedner (2007) suggested that there are two opposing schools of thought. The first believes that if there is absolute certainty of the alleged offence occurring, then punishment today is just as valid as waiting until after the event. On the other hand, up until the actual commission of the act, a so-called window of opportunity exists, allowing the individual to refrain until the last minute. In fact, Lendermann (2009) warned that by moving the *actus reus* forward along the axis to include preparatory offences, the motivation to abandon the terrorist act is greatly reduced. While these debates may appear somewhat philosophical, there are examples outside of the terrorism context that can be used to contextualise the debate, as discussed in the following section.

2.4 Other Pre-emptive Measures

The notion of trying to pre-empt crime is neither novel nor exclusive to anti-terrorism (Bronitt 2003). For instance, the practice of 'binding over', a precautionary measure to prevent future crime, dates back to the fourteenth century.[25] This practice, although originating in civil law, can incur criminal sanctions if not adhered to (Bronitt and McSherry 2005). However, it is worth noting that the court requires admissible evidence that without the order, there is a real risk of a breach of the peace occurring (Crown Prosecution Service 2009). A modern and frequently cited example of a preventive order is the Anti-Social Behaviour Order (ASBO) in the United Kingdom (Ashworth 2009; Macdonald 2007).[26] An ASBO is a civil preventive order which aims to protect people or entire neighbourhoods from intimidating and anti-social behaviour rather than punishing the culprit for it (Home Office). However, a breach of the conditions of the order constitutes a criminal offence punishable by up to five years in prison. The relevant standard of proof is that of *beyond reasonable doubt* due to its quasi-criminal nature, as opposed to the civil standard of *balance of probabilities* in binding over or civil orders (Bronitt and McSherry 2005). While the Labour government insisted ASBOs were only ever issued in exceptional circumstances, their large number (17,000 between 1999 and 2008) and the fact that they were issued in response to a wide range of behaviours and offences such as prostitution, casts doubt on that assertion. There are examples of other applications of preventive laws, such as domestic violence orders and the recently introduced orders to control outlaw motorcycle gangs in South Australia, New South Wales and the Northern Territory.[27]

---

[25] *Justice of the Peace Act* 1361.

[26] For a direct comparison between control orders and the ABSO, see Stuart Macdonald (2007).

[27] *Serious and Organised Crime (Control) Act 2008* (SA), *Criminal Organisations Legislation Amendment Act 2009* (NSW), *Serious Crime Control Act 2009* (NT).

While punishment and detention are most frequently associated with criminal law, there are civil law provisions that allow for the detention of individuals against their will prior to committing an offence. Preventive measures have long been used to deal with public order offences, such as controlling inebriates and unruly teenagers. Article 5(1)(e) of the European Convention on Human Rights (ECHR) states that the detention of persons of unsound mind, alcoholics, drug addicts or vagrants, as well as to prevent spreading of infectious diseases, is considered lawful. Involuntary detention is justified in cases where the aim is treatment or where there is at risk of harming themselves or others, in the case of mental illness, for example, or indeed to prevent the spread of infectious disease (McSherry 2002). Contemporary mental health legislation originated out of the state's desire to protect its citizens from dangerous acts (Finnane 1981; Garton 1988; Moran 1985; Walker 1968). Its rationale is founded both in treatment and protecting the community.[28]

Not all preventive measures sit outside the criminal law framework. Control order cases have also seen several comparisons made to preventive measures within criminal law, such as bail applications, indefinite sentences, parole and probation (McSherry 2002).

Outside the security context, the threshold for pre-emptive measures in the criminal justice process is related to dangerousness and how it related to risky individuals and groups, some of which were to be controlled to preserve the political status quo (McCulloch and Pickering 2009; Pratt 1997). Preventive legislation has been introduced to supervise and, in exceptional cases, even preventively detain offenders perceived as being particularly dangerous or risky upon their release from prison to prevent recidivism (Keyzer and Blay 2006; Mercado and Ogloff 2007). In keeping with the actuarial trend in criminal justice,[29] offenders are risk-assessed prior to release to determine their risk of re-offending. An important distinction between these and other preventive measures is that they target convicted offenders upon the completion of their served sentence. A commonly cited example is the serious sex offender legislation enacted in the United States, Canada, New Zealand, and most Australian states.[30] A variety of conditions tailored to the offender's circumstances may be imposed by the court, including treatment, limitations on employment, curfews or prohibiting contact with certain individuals (Wood and Ogloff 2006). Any breach constitutes an indictable offence. In more serious cases, offenders may be detained indefinitely, the justification

---

[28] In Australia, the balance between public protection and taking into account the mentally ill person's rights varies between states (McSherry 2002; Rangarajan and McSherry 2009). McSherry has highlighted that all Australian jurisdictions have review mechanisms in place concerning the involuntary committal of individuals with mental illnesses. However, jurisdictions vary greatly on the type of order under which someone is detained, either through administrative power or by judicial order.

[29] Actuarial justice focuses on evaluating future risks and is often associated with dangerousness or treatment programs (see Sect. 5.2).

[30] QLD, NSW, SA, Vic, and WA.

being the prevention of highly likely future offending and thus, the protection of the community. Pratt described extended sentences as ushering in a new penal concept, one where sanctions could be imposed without committing an offence (Pratt 1997, p. 58). Despite the imposition of such measures on a convicted offender, serious concerns with regard to human rights have been raised, not least since these intensive supervision orders may last for up to 15 years in some states.[31] Served in the community, these intensive supervision orders impose similar restrictions to control orders on the individuals, including curfews, restrictions on movement and employment and electronic tagging (Wood and Ogloff 2006). Opponents of such measures argue that the principles of due process are not observed, since the offender, having served his or her sentence, is subjected to further supervision or detention.

2.4.1 Evidence of Future Offending

Detaining individuals for the purposes of prevention highlights the difficulties in making predictions about the future likelihood of offending and the associated difficulty with addressing uncertain anticipated risk and harm. Unlike control orders, preventive detention of sex offenders and in mental illness cases relies on expert medical opinions to support assertions of future risk of the individuals in question (McSherry 2006; Mercado and Ogloff 2007). One might argue that the severity of detention makes the inclusion of expert evidence paramount. While the underlying aim of these measures is to protect the population, McSherry (2006) argued that the rationale of protecting the community is often based on vague and flawed assessments of risk, and should not be the justification for deprivation of liberty, making judicial review essential. Even predictions based on extensive expert testimony have been found to be "prone to very significant degrees of error when matched against actuality" (Stephens J in Veen (No 1) at 464, quoted in McSherry 2002, p. 38).[32] Moreover, studies show that preventive laws have only a minor impact on the total number of sexual offences (McSherry and Keyzer 2009; Mercado and Ogloff 2007; Wood and Ogloff 2006). This may in part be due to the limited application of such laws, which were never intended to be applied broadly, but only in exceptional cases.

Given the difficulties associated with predicting future behaviour, even when reviewed by relevant experts, ensuring the proportionality of preventive measures becomes increasingly complicated. To overcome the traditionally reactive principle of proportionality, Zedner (2007) proposed a two-tiered approach to

---

[31] In Victoria, orders and recidivism risk are revised every 3 years. If after 15 years the individual is still considered high risk, a further supervision order for an additional 15 years may be applied for.

[32] *Veen (No 1)* (1979) 143 CLR 458; and *Veen (No 2)* (1988) 164 CLR 465.

pre-punishment proportionality, one which goes beyond the current standard of proof of having reasonable suspicion about the potential risk posed by a particular individual: assessing the severity of the anticipated/threatened harm, as well as the likelihood of the event/harm actually occurring. Furthermore, she argued that the greater the impact of preventive detention (or obligations) on an individual, the greater the need for evidence of actual dangerousness. To ensure continued proportionality, Zedner stressed the need for continued review of the risk posed by controlees to see if the restrictions set out in the order are still needed. However, this appears difficult to do in practice if the pre-emptive measures are actually effective in preventing the anticipated events; only the lifting of restrictions could highlight new/continued risks posed by that individual. Proportionality is difficult to determine if the risk is uncertain. It is important to highlight at this point that these challenges are also inherent in non-terrorist related instances. Parole boards and mental health tribunals, for instance, are required to make such judgements on a daily basis.

2.5 Reacting to Prevention

Much of the debate around control orders stems from their hybrid nature, thus not fitting neatly into our preconceived categories about the division of responsibilities between the Executive and Judiciary, and civil and criminal frameworks. Moreover, their preventive intent aimed at protecting the public from a terrorist attack appears to have circumvented some of the standards against which such measures should be evaluated. Although control orders incorporate more judicial elements than previous executive measures, they still struggle to adhere to the conventional standards of the criminal process. Being civil measures they are not required to meet the more stringent safeguards.

However, several arguments have been put forward as to why control orders should nonetheless adhere to the safeguards enshrined in international conventions. Considerable restrictions and obligations, tantamount to house arrest in some British cases, were imposed on the basis of potentially unsound intelligence of which the controlee was not informed, rather than on evidence capable of standing up to scrutiny in a court of law. Procedural safeguards designed to ensure a fair trial were thus compromised. Given the severity of some of the conditions, the line between punishment and prevention becomes blurred. Simply introducing a preventive rationale into a civil measure does not automatically make it less punitive (Zedner 2007, 2009b). Moreover, breaching any of the preventively imposed obligations might lead to a criminal charge resulting in imprisonment.

Despite Pratt's assertion that the introduction of indeterminate sentences ushered in the beginning of prevention of future crime, the interventions introduced to control these offenders are applied *after* sentencing for violent and sexual crimes or after repeat offending, the aim being to prevent further offending, i.e. recidivism. There is a clear distinction between individuals who are either having an existing sentence extended or are required to adhere to restrictions upon their release from prison, i.e. where preventive measures are applied in reaction to an offence, reactive prevention; and those who are detained or restricted on mere suspicion without any prior finding of guilt, i.e. pre-emptive prevention. One aims to prevent an individual from re-offending upon completion of a served sentence, i.e. post-crime, while the other aims to prevent them from potentially offending at some point in the future, without necessarily having offended in the past, i.e. being purely pre-emptive. The difference between reactive and pre-emptive prevention is illustrated below.

Figure 2.1, referred to as axis of prevention, represents time. A crime is committed in Fig. 2.1a. The criminal justice system is inherently reactive in nature, so it typically intervenes *after* the commission of the offence. Preventive legislation however gives a state the power to intervene prior to an offence being committed to prevent it from (re-)occurring. For example, it might be used preventively to detain offenders perceived as being particularly dangerous or risky upon their release from prison to prevent recidivism, for example sex offenders. Dershowitz (2006) called this the injury or harm approach to crime control. An important distinction between these and other preventive measures is that they target convicted offenders upon the completion of their served sentence. This then can be described as *reactive prevention.* At this end of the spectrum, there is greater reliance on evidence, as a crime has already been committed and the individual found guilty. The risk of future offending is calculated based on previous events.

We have established that there are incidents where the intervention takes place prior to the commission of the crime, where having the criminal intent to carry out a crime is a crime in itself. These are known as inchoate offences and include attempt, incitement, conspiracy, as well as a wide range of statutory preparatory offences, illustrated in Fig. 2.1b. Akin to Dershowitz's dangerous act approach, the actus reus does not need to have happened, rather, there was evidence of dangerousness or intent, such as in the case of dangerous driving or attempted murder.

The precautionary logic, however, takes this rationale even further, as no evidence of dangerousness is required prior to intervening. Pre-emptive or

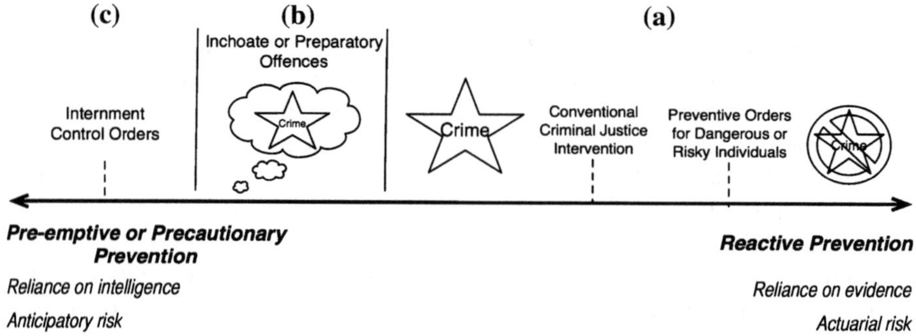

Fig. 2.1 The axis of prevention

precautionary anti-terrorism legislation, such as control orders and internment, for example, thus differ not only from the reactive preventive measures we have just seen, but go even beyond inchoate offences. What Dershowitz called the dangerous person approach, I call pre-emptive or precautionary prevention, illustrated in Fig. 2.1c. It is with this distinction in mind that the rest of the Brief has been analysed and written.

To summarise, the literature on control orders has focused on three key points: Firstly, control orders are hybrid measures which exist outside of the traditional legal frameworks, enabling departures from well established procedural safeguards in criminal cases. Secondly, these deviations are justified on the basis of the exceptional risk posed by terrorism and the need to protect the state and its people from a terrorist attack. Finally, given that control orders are issued on the basis of anticipated risk rather than reacting to an actual act that has already occurred, they appear to constitute a more pre-emptive species of preventive order compared to the more reactively preventive ones. Having identified the central arguments against these measures, I now turn to examine the legal framework of control orders and their practical application. The following two chapters provide a detailed analysis of the statutory provisions giving rise to the control order scheme in the UK and Australia, as well as a comprehensive examination of their implementations in both jurisdictions.

References

Appleby, G., & Williams, J. (2010). The anti-terror creep: law and order, the states and the high court of Australia. In N. McGarrity, A. Lynch, & G. Williams (Eds.), *Counter-terrorism and beyond: the culture of law and justice after 9/11*. London: Routledge.

Ashworth, A. (2000). Is the criminal law a lost cause? *Law Quarterly Review, 116*(2), 225–256.

Ashworth, A. (2002). Sentencing. In M. Maguire, R. Morgan, & R. Reiner (Eds.), *The oxford handbook of criminology* (3rd ed., pp. 1076–1112). Oxford: Oxford University Press.

Ashworth, A. (2005). *Sentencing and criminal justice* (4th ed.). Cambridge: Cambridge University Press.

Ashworth, A. (2006). Four threats to the presumption of innocence. *The International Journal of Evidence and Proof, 10*(4), 241–279.

Ashworth, A., & Zedner, L. (2007). Defending the criminal law: reflections on the changing character of crime, procedure, and sanctions. *Criminal Law and Philosophy, 2*(1), 21–51.

Ashworth, A. (2009). Criminal law, human rights and preventative justice. In B. McSherry, A. Norrie, & S. Bronitt (Eds.), *Regulating deviance: the redirection of criminalisation and the futures of criminal law*. Oxford and Portland OR: Hart Publishing.

Ashworth, A., & Zedner, L. (2010). Preventive orders: a problem of undercriminalization? In R. A. Duff, L. Farmer, S. Marshall, M. Renzo, & V. Tadros (Eds.), *The boundaries of the criminal law*. Oxford: Oxford University Press.

Australian Law Reform Commission. (2003). *Principled Regulation: Federal Civil & Administrative Penalties in Australia*. Sydney: ALRC.

Bonner, D. (1992). United Kingdom: the United Kingdom response to terrorism. *Terrorism and Political Violence, 4*(4), 171–205.

Bonner, D. (2006). Checking the executive? Detention without trial, control orders, due process and human rights. *European Public Law, 12*(1), 45–71.

Bonner, D. (2007). *Executive measures, terrorism and national security: have the rules of the game changed?* Aldershot: Ashgate.
Bronitt, S. (2003). *Australia's legal response to terrorism: neither novel nor extraordinary?* Paper presented at the Castan Centre for human rights law conference "Human Rights 2003: The Year in Review", Melbourne.
Bronitt, S., & McSherry, B. (2005). *Principles of criminal law.* Sydney: Lawbook Co.
Bronitt, S. (2008). Balancing security and liberty: critical perspectives on terrorism law reform. In M. Gani & P. Mathew (Eds.), *Fresh perspectives on the war on terror.* Canberra: ANU E Press.
Bronitt, S., & McSherry, B. (2010). *Principles of criminal law* (3rd edn.). Sydney: Thomson Reuters (Professional) Australia Limited.
Bronitt, S., & Donkin, S. (2012). Australian responses to 9/11: New world legal hybrids? In A. Masferrer (Ed.), *Post 9/11 and the State of Permanent Legal Emergency* (Vol. 14, pp. 223–239). Dordrecht: Springer Netherlands.
Blackstone, W. (1769). *Commentaries on the laws of England* (Vol. 4). Oxford: Clarendon Press.
Carlile, A., Berriew, B. (2006). First report of the independent reviewer pursuant to section 14(3) of the prevention of terrorism act 2005. London: HMSO.
Carlile, A., Berriew, B. (2011). sixth report of the independent reviewer pursuant to section 14(3) of the prevention of terrorism act 2005. London: HMSO.
Crawford, A. (2006). Networked governance and the post-regulatory state? Steering, rowing and anchoring the provision of policing and security. *Theoretical Criminology, 10*(4), 449–479.
Cohen, S. (1979). The punitive city: notes on the dispersal of social control. *Crime, Law and Social Change, 3*(4), 339–363. doi:10.1007/bf00729115.
Cornall, R. (2007). The effectiveness of criminal laws on terrorism. In A. Lynch, E. MacDonald, & G. Williams (Eds.), *Law and liberty in the war on terror.* Sydney: Federation Press.
Crown Prosecution Service. (2009). *Ancillary orders & powers: prosecutors' toolkit.* London: CPS.
Cotterrell, R. (1992). *The sociology of law: an introduction* (2nd ed.). London: Butterworths.
Dershowitz, A. M. (2006). *Preemption: a knife that cuts both ways.* New York: W.W. Norton & Company.
Duff, A., & Garland, D. (1994). *A reader on punishment.* Oxford: Oxford University Press.
Dyzenhaus, D., & Thwaites, R. (2007). Legality and emergency—the judiciary in a time of terror. In A. Lynch, E. MacDonald, & G. Williams (Eds.), *Law and liberty in the war on terror.* Sydney: The Federation Press.
Ericson, R. V. (2007). *Crime in an insecure world.* Cambridge: Polity Press.
Finnane, M. (1981). *Insanity and the insane in post-famine Ireland.* London: Croom Helm.
Finnane, M., & Donkin, S. (2013). Fighting terror with law? Some other genealogies of pre-emption. *International Journal for Crime and Justice, 2*(1), 3–17.
Garton, S. (1988). *Medicine & madness: a social history of insanity in New South Wales 1880–1940.* Kensington: New South Wales University Press.
Harris Rimmer, S. (2010). A passport to punishment: administrative measures of control for national security purposes. In N. McGarrity, A. Lynch, & G. Williams (Eds.), *Counter-terrorism and beyond: the culture of law and justice after 9/11.* London: Routledge.
Hudson, B. (2002). Punishment and control. In M. Maguire, R. Morgan, & R. Reiner (Eds.), *The oxford handbook of criminology* (3rd ed.). Oxford: Oxford University Press.
Ip, J. (2007). Comparative perspectives on the detention of terrorist suspects. *Transnational law & contemporary problems, 16*, 773–871.
International Commission of Jurists. (2009). Assessing damage, urging action: report of the eminent jurists panel on terrorism, counter-terrorism and human rights. In I. C. O. Jurists (Ed.). Geneva: International Commission of Jurists.
Joint Committee on Human Rights. (2005). Prevention of terrorism bill—tenth report of session 2004–2005. London: HMSO.

Joint Committee on Human Rights. (2006). *Twelfth report of session 2005-06: Counter-terrorism policy and human rights: draft prevention of terrorism act 2005 (Continuance in force of sections 1 to 9) Order 2006*. London: HMSO.

Kavanagh, A. (2010). Special advocates, control orders and the right to a fair trial. *The Modern Law Review, 73*(5), 824–857.

Keyzer, P., & Blay, S. (2006). Double punishment—preventive detention schemes under Australian legislation and their consistency with international law: the Fardon communication commentary. *Melbourne journal of international law, 7*(2), 407–424.

Lacey, N. (2002). Legal constructions of crime. In M. Maguire, R. Morgan, & R. Reiner (Eds.), *The oxford handbook of criminology* (3rd ed., pp. 264–285). Oxford: Oxford University Press.

Lendermann, M. (2009). Prävention durch Recht—Kann normative auf Terrorismus reagiert werden? [Prevention through law: can one react normatively to terrorism?]. *Humbolt Forum Recht* (12), 163–175.

Lynch, A., & Williams, G. (2006). *What price security? Taking stock of Australia's anti-terror laws*. Sydney: University of New South Wales Press Ltd.

Lynch, A. (2006a). Legislating with urgency—the enactment of the anti-terrorism act [No 1] 2005. *Melbourne University Law Review 30*(3), 747–781.

Lynch, A. (2006b). Maximising the drama: 'Jihad Jack', the court of appeal and the Australian media. *Adelaide Law Review, 27*, 311–334.

Lynch, A., McGarrity, N., & Williams, G. (2010). The emergence of a 'culture of control'. In N. McGarrity, A. Lynch, & G. Williams (Eds.), *Counter-terrorism and beyond: the culture of law and justice after 9/11*. London: Routledge.

Macdonald, S. (2007). ASBOs and control orders: two recurring themes, two apparent contradictions. *Parliamentary Affairs, 60*(4), 601–624.

Manningham-Buller, E. (2005). *The International Terrorist Threat and the dilemmas in countering it*. Speech by The Director General of the Security Service, Dame Eliza Manningham-Buller, At The Ridderzaal, Binnenhof, The Hague, Netherlands, 1 Sept 2005, from https://www.mi5.gov.uk/output/director-generals-speech-to-the-aivd-2005.html.

Mazerolle, L., & Ransley, J. (2005). *Third party policing*. Cambridge: Cambridge University Press.

McCulloch, J., & Carlton, B. (2006). Preempting justice: suppression of financing of terrorism and the war on terror. *Current Issues in Criminal Justice, 17*, 397.

McCulloch, J., & Pickering, S. (2009). Pre-crime and counter-terrorism: imagining future crime in the 'war on terror'. *British Journal of Criminology, 49*, 628–645.

McCulloch, J., & Pickering, S. (2010). Counter-terrorism: the law and policing of pre-emption. In N. McGarrity, A. Lynch, & G. Williams (Eds.), *Counter-terrorism and beyond: the culture of law and justice after 9/11*. London: Routledge.

McSherry, B. (2002). *Risk assessment by mental health professionals and the prevention of future violent behaviour*. Canberra: Criminology Research Council.

McSherry, B. (2004). Terrorism offences in the criminal code: broadening the boundaries of Australian criminal laws. *University of New South Wales Law Journal, 27*(2), 354–372.

McSherry, B. (2006). Sex, drugs and 'evil' souls: the growing reliance on preventive detention regimes. *Monash University Law Review, 32*(2), 237–274.

McSherry, B., & Keyzer, P. (2009). *Sex offenders and preventive detention: politics, policy and practice*. Sydney: The Federation Press.

Mercado, C. C., & Ogloff, J. R. P. (2007). Risk and the preventive detention of sex offenders in Australia and the United States. *International Journal of Law and Psychiatry, 30*(1), 49–59.

Metcalfe, E. (2009). *Secret evidence*. London: Justice.

Moran, R. (1985). The modern foundation for the insanity defense: the cases of James Hadfield (1800) and Daniel McNaughtan (1843). *Annals of the American Academy of Political and Social Science, 477*(1), 31–42.

Pickering, S., McCulloch, J., & Wright-Neville, D. (2008). *Counter-terrorism policing: community, cohesion and security*. New York: Springer.

Pratt, J. (1997). *Governing the dangerous: dangerousness, law and social change*. Sydney: The Federation Press.

Press Association. (2003). MI5 warns major terror attack is 'only a matter of time'. *The Guardian*. 17 June 2003, Retrieved from http://www.guardian.co.uk/uk/2003/jun/17/alqaida.terrorism?INTCMP=SRCH.

Ramsay, P. (2009). The theory of vulnerable autonomy and the legitimacy of civil preventative orders. In B. McSherry, A. Norrie, & S. Bronitt (Eds.), *Regulating deviance: the redirection of criminalisation and the futures of criminal law*. Oxford and Portland OR: Hart Publishing.

Rangarajan, S., & McSherry, B. (2009). To detain or not to detain: a question of public duty? *Psychiatry, Psychology & Law, 16*, 288–302.

Ransley, J., & Donkin, S. (2009). *Law in order: interpreting Australian anti-terrorism legislation*. Paper presented at the Crossing Borders: Promoting Regional Law Enforcement Cooperation—European, Australian and Asia-Pacific Perspectives, Canberra, 8 April 2009, Canberra.

Roach, K. (2002). Did September 11 change everything? Struggling to preserve Canadian values in the face of terrorism. *McGill Law Journal, 47*, 893–947.

Roach, K. (2010). The eroding distinction between intelligence and evidence in terrorism investigations. In N. McGarrity, A. Lynch, & G. Williams (Eds.), *Counter-terrorism and beyond: the culture of law and justice after 9/11*. London: Routledge.

Ruddock, P. (2007). Law as a preventative weapon against terrorism. In A. Lynch, E. MacDonald, & G. Williams (Eds.), *Law and liberty in the war on terror*. Sydney: Federation Press.

Simcox, R. (2010). *Control orders: strengthening national security*. London: The Centre for Social Cohesion.

Spjut, R. J. (1986). Internment and detention without trial in Northern Ireland 1971–1975: ministerial policy and practice. *The Modern Law Review, 49*(6), 712–740.

The Street Review. (2008). The street review: a review of interoperability between the AFP and its national security partners. In L. Street, M. Brady, & M. Moroney (Eds.). Canberra.

von Hirsch, A. (1990). The ethics of community-based sanctions. *Crime & Delinquency, 36*(1), 162–173. doi:10.1177/0011128790036001011.

Walker, N. (1968). *Crime and insanity in England*. Edinburgh: University Press.

Walker, N. (1982). Unscientific, unwise, unprofitable or unjust? *British Journal of Criminology, 22*(3), 276–284.

Walker, C. (1992). *The prevention of terrorism in British law* (2nd ed.). Manchester: Manchester University Press.

Walker, C. (2004). Terrorism and criminal justice: past, present and future. *Criminal Law Review*, 311–327.

Walker, C. (2011). *Terrorism and the Law*. Oxford: Oxford University Press.

White, M. (2007). A judicial perspective—the making of preventative detention orders. In A. Lynch, E. MacDonald, & G. Williams (Eds.), *Law and liberty in the war on terror*. Sydney: Federation Press.

Wood, M., & Ogloff, J. R. P. (2006). Victoria's serious sex offenders monitoring act 2005: implications for the accuracy of sex offender risk assessment. *Psychiatry, Psychology and Law, 13*(2), 182–198.

Zedner, L. (2005). Securing liberty in the face of terror: reflections from criminal justice. *Journal of Law and Society, 32*(4), 507–533.

Zedner, L. (2007). Preventive justice or pre-punishment? The case of control orders. *Current Legal Problems, 60*(1), 174–203. doi:10.1093/clp/60.1.174.

Zedner, L. (2009a). Fixing the future? The pre-emptive turn in criminal justice. In B. McSherry, A. Norrie, & S. Bronitt (Eds.), *Regulating deviance: the redirection of criminalisation and the futures of criminal law*. Oxford and Portland OR: Hart Publishing.

Zedner, L. (2009b). *Security*. Abingdon: Routledge.

Chapter 3
The Legal Framework

3.1 Introduction

The aim of this chapter is to conduct a statutory analysis of the legislation providing the legal framework for control orders. I begin by providing a brief account of the developments immediately preceding the introduction of the control order regime in the United Kingdom, before providing an overview of the provisions contained within the *Prevention of Terrorism Act (PTA) 2005*, describing the two types of control orders and the procedure involved in issuing them. The same procedure is then repeated for the Australian *Anti-Terrorism Act (No. 2) 2005*, highlighting similarities and divergences between the two statutory instruments.

The United Kingdom has a long history of dealing with terrorism through law, be it administrative or criminal, both reactively and pre-emptively. In the wake of 9/11, Parliament hastily introduced further legislation, the *Anti-Terrorism, Crime and Security Act 2001* (ATCSA) (Macdonald 2007). Its most controversial provision enabled the Home Secretary to detain foreign nationals suspected of terrorism, indefinitely and without charge or trial.[1] Appeals, only able to be taken on decisions on points of law, were limited to a closed Special Immigration Appeals Commission (SIAC). Other powers included granting the police and security services,[2] the power to request disclosure of personal records by public bodies, including schools, hospitals, and Inland Revenue, in terrorism and criminal investigations; freezing of assets of terrorist suspects by both law enforcement agencies and the Treasury; introducing new offences related to chemical, nuclear or biological weapons; requiring transport carriers to disclose passenger information; communication service providers to retain and make available their data; and finally, obliging financial institutions to flag any suspected terrorist financing

---

1 See for example Shah (2005) for a more in depth analysis of the ATCSA 2001.

2 Including foreign agencies.

S. Donkin, *Preventing Terrorism and Controlling Risk*, Springer Briefs in International and Comparative Criminology, DOI: 10.1007/978-1-4614-8705-0_3,

to law enforcement agencies. However, a committee of Law Lords in *A and others v Secretary of State for the Home Department*[3] held that Part IV of the ATCSA 2001, i.e. the power to indefinitely detain foreign nationals suspected of posing a terrorist threat without trial, was incompatible with the European Convention on Human Rights.[4] The Law Lords found the powers to be discriminatory against foreign nationals, and a disproportionate response to the level of threat[5] (Mcdonald 2007). Within three months of the judgment, the government passed the *Prevention of Terrorism Act (PTA) 2005*, replacing the unlawful detention[6] with a two-tiered control order regime in March 2005. Unlike the previous measures, however, control orders are not limited to foreign nationals. The Home Secretary described them as a mechanism to contain and disrupt individuals who can neither be prosecuted nor deported.[7]

To recap briefly, the aim of control orders is to protect the general public from a risk of terrorism by imposing obligations on individuals who are suspected of involvement in terrorist-related activities so as to restrict or prevent these individuals from further involvement in said activities.[8] Control orders are technically civil measures, although a breach of an obligation constitutes a criminal offence, punishable with up to five years imprisonment. They are issued by a court at the request of the Home Secretary. The burden of proof for the non-derogating control order is not the traditional civil one of *on the balance of probabilities*, but an even lesser standard of *reasonable ground for suspicion.*

A few months after their inception in the UK, Australia also introduced control orders as part of its extensive new anti-terrorism legislation. However, the British and Australian provisions differ significantly on the severity of restrictions, principally due to the Australian scheme not providing for detention of the individual. The next section examines the British legislation and its provision for both derogating and non-derogating varieties of control orders. The control order scheme was eventually abolished in December 2011 and replaced with Terrorism Prevention and Investigations Measures (TPIMs), retaining many of the controversial aspects outlined below.

---

[3] (2004) UKHL 56 and (2005) 2 WLR 87 available at http://www.parliament.the-stationery-office.co.uk/pa/ld200405/ldjudgmt/jd041216/a&oth-1.htm.

[4] For an in-depth overview of the history and run up to *A (FC) and others (FC) v Secretary of State for the Home Department* (2004) UKHL 56, see Bonner (2006) pp. 53–59.

[5] H.C. Deb., Vol. 430, col. 305 (26 January 2005).

[6] The PTA 2005 repealed s 21 to s 32 of the ATCSA 2001, repealed s62(15) and (16) and Sch. 7 para 30 of the *Nationality, Immigration and Asylum Act 2002*, as well as amending several other statutes, including the *Terrorism Act 2000.*

[7] H.C. Deb., Vol. 430, col. 307 (26 January 2005).

[8] PTA, s1 (1) and (3).

3.2 British Control Orders: The Origin of Two Species

The *Prevention of Terrorism Act* (*PTA*) *2005* set out two types of control order, namely the derogating and the non-derogating order. The distinction by derogation pertained to the UK's obligations as a signatory of the European Convention on Human Rights (ECHR), whereby Article 5 prohibits the detention of an individual without due process of law. Prior to a control order of either type being made, the Home Secretary was required to liaise with the police to determine whether there was sufficient evidence against that individual to be used for the purposes of prosecution.[9] Throughout the duration of the control order, the police were required to continually review the individual's conduct with a view of prosecution.[10] Given that only non-derogating orders were ever issued, this Brief focuses on this type only.

3.2.1 The Non-Derogating Control Order

A non-derogating control order (NDCO) severely *restricted* an individual's liberty by imposing a range of conditions on a person suspected of involvement in terrorism. Section 1(3) stated:

> The obligations that may be imposed by a control order made against an individual are any obligations that the Secretary of State or (as the case may be) the court considers necessary for purposes connected with preventing or restricting involvement by that individual in terrorism-related activity.

In practice, obligations translated to restrictions on the controlee's belongings, activities, ways of earning a living, association, place of residence and who was allowed to enter it, imposition of curfews, travel restrictions (including surrendering his or her passport), and having to report at particular times and places, to name but a few. For instance, whether or not the controlee was required to be electronically tagged was at the Home Secretary's discretion.

As for the alleged involvement in terrorism-related activity, it not only covered the more commonly assumed stages of an offence, i.e. commission, preparation or instigation,[11] but any conduct facilitating, intending to facilitate or encouraging either of those stages, as well as assisting individuals who are or are suspected of being involved in any terrorism-related activity.[12] Examples of such offences

---

[9] S 8(2).

[10] S 8(4).

[11] S 1(9)(a).

[12] S 1(9)(b–d) respectively.

include writing, publishing or distributing material glorifying terrorism; publicly advocating or preaching, and encouraging others to commit terrorist acts.[13]

3.2.1.1 Issuance of NDCO

Section 2(1) stated that a NDCO could be issued by the Home Secretary if he/she

(a) has reasonable grounds for suspecting that the individual is or has been involved in terrorism-related activity; and
(b) considers that it is necessary, for purposes connected with protecting members of the public from a risk of terrorism, to make a control order imposing obligations on that individual.

A non-derogating control order was in effect for twelve months, and could be renewed for the duration for which the Home Secretary (HS) believed s 2(1) still applied.[14] Once a NDCO was issued, it needed to be approved by a High Court judge within seven days.[15] The court's function was to determine whether the grounds on which the HS had put forward the proposal were "obviously flawed"(s 3(2)(a)). If it considered the proposal viable, a hearing had to be set up. However, the individual in question was not required/permitted to be present in court (*ex parte*), nor notified of the application being made, nor given the chance to represent himself.[16] If the court found flaws in the HS's reasoning, or the obligations proposed, the order or that particular obligation had to be overturned, otherwise, the order had to be confirmed.[17] Upon confirmation, the individual in question was notified of the order made against him.[18] As for what constituted flaws in the HS's reasoning, the PTA set out that "the principles applicable on an application for judicial review" applied,[19] i.e. illegality, procedural impropriety and irrationality, the so-called Diplock Trilogy (Bonner 2006). In other words, the court had the power to overturn the use of executive powers if they violated basic judicial principles such as due process in a particular case.

Obligations set out in the original NDCO could be modified, both at the suggestion of the controlee, or the HS.[20] The HS could also decide to revoke a

---

[13] Since the introduction of the PTA in 2005, two new acts were introduced, both slightly amending the control order regime. Firstly, the *Terrorism Act 2006* created new preparatory terrorism offences, including encouragement of terrorism (s1), dissemination of terrorist publications (s2), preparation of terrorist acts (s5) and training for terrorism (s6). The creation of these new offences enabled individuals who might otherwise have been subject to a control order to be charged and prosecuted in criminal proceedings.

[14] Ibid, s 2(4) and (6).

[15] Ibid, s 3(1)(a) and 3(4).

[16] Ibid, s 3(5)(a), (b) and (c) respectively.

[17] Ibid, s 3(6).

[18] Ibid, s 3(9).

[19] Ibid, s3(11).

[20] S 7(1).

NDCO.[21] Interestingly, s2(9) highlighted that all the imposed obligations did not have to relate to preventing the event for which the individual came under suspicion in the first place—in effect, giving the Home Secretary somewhat of a carte blanche to impose additional restrictions.

As previously stated, although the control order was a civil measure, any breach of obligation left the controlee open to criminal prosecution. Section 9(1) stated:

> (1) A person who, without reasonable excuse, contravenes an obligation imposed on him by a control order is guilty of an offence.

Further, more specific breaches were outlined in subsequent sections of the PTA, such as re-entering the United Kingdom after the expiry of an order,[22] not reporting to a specified person,[23] or obstructing a designated person from entering his or her house.[24] If the controlee was found guilty, he faced imprisonment for up to five years and/or a fine.[25]

3.2.2 *Appeal Process*

A controlee could appeal if their NDCO was renewed, or his or her obligations were amended without notification. Section 10(1)(b) actually stated "an obligation imposed by such an order has been modified *without the consent* of the controlled person" but I would assume most controlees didn't actually consent to any of these restrictions being imposed on them (without due process). The function of the court in such cases was identical to the initial hearing, where it had to determine any flaws in the Home Secretary's reasoning and to prevent the controlee from engaging in terrorism-related activities.[26] Had his or her reasoning been flawed, the court had the power to (a) quash the renewal; (b) quash one or more obligations imposed by the order; or (c) give directions to the Home Secretary to revoke the order or to modify its obligations.[27] Otherwise, the appeal had to be dismissed. Finally, section 11(1) stated that control order decisions could only be questioned in court or on appeal from court.

Due to the ATCSA 2001 focus on deporting foreign suspects, an appeal process to the Special Immigration Appeals Tribunal (SIAC) was introduced, subsequently amending the tribunal's operation (Smith 2007). Although control order cases were heard by the High Court, the sensitive nature of the supporting materials led

---

[21] S 7(2).

[22] S 9(2)(b).

[23] S 9(2)(d).

[24] S 9(3).

[25] S 9(4)(a).

[26] S 10(4) and (5).

[27] S 10(7).

to SIAC procedures being adopted by the High Court,[28] incorporating measures of non-disclosure of sensitive information, closed proceedings and the appointment of Special Advocates (Bonner 2007; Ip 2007; Walker 2011). The use of Special Advocates in control order proceedings has, according to Walker, been controversial not least due to their mandated limited interaction with the suspect prior to hearing the sensitive evidence. Bonner (2007) highlighted that even though their appointment is discretionary, only material disclosed to a Special Advocate on behalf of the appellant can be relied upon, making their appointment a formality. However, once they have seen the closed material, they are prohibited from any further contact with the appellant or their legal representation. The transferral of SIAC rules to the High Court also means it is no longer obligated to adhere to the same rules of evidence of a traditional court of law, be it criminal or civil (Bonner 2007), leading the former Shadow Home Secretary to describe the process as "Kafkaesque".[29]

In summary then, the British control order system, despite not having resorted to derogations under emergency provisions, was not only a hybrid between the civil and the criminal systems, but also incorporated proceedings based on immigration administration, which had a significant effect on the issuance of control orders. Before examining some of the practical issues created by the statutory framework, the next section examines the Australian adaptation of the control order scheme.

3.3 Australian Adaptation of Control Orders

The Australian system of control orders was introduced as part of the *Anti-Terrorism Act (No. 2) 2005*,[30] imposing a variety of obligations, prohibitions and restrictions on a person[31] suspected of posing a terrorist threat for up to twelve months at a time. The object of the act is to protect the public from a terrorist act.[32] Since Australia is not accountable to the ECHR, unlike its British predecessor there is only one type of control order, but it involves a two-stage process of interim and confirmed control orders, both of which are examined in turn.

---

[28] The Civil Procedure (Amendment No. 2) Rules 2005, S.I. 2005/656, introducing part 76 of the *Civil Procedure Rules 1998*.

[29] H.C. Deb., Vol. 430, col. 310 (26 January 2005).

[30] The same act also introduced preventative detention orders, stop and search powers, amended sedition offences and made changes to ASIO powers and financial reporting obligations, amongst other things.

[31] For adults; and up to three months for people aged 16–18.

[32] 104.1.

3.3.1 The Interim Control Order

In circumstances where the Australian Federal Police (AFP) either

(a) considers on reasonable grounds that the order in the terms to be requested would substantially assist in preventing a terrorist act; or
(b) suspects on reasonable grounds that the person has provided training to, or received training from, a listed terrorist organisation,[33]

a senior member of the AFP requests the Attorney General's (AG) written consent to apply for an interim control order (iCO) to be made against a suspect. Making the request, the AFP must include a prepared draft of the iCO, on what grounds the order is sought, including any arguments against making such an order.[34] Furthermore, each obligation needs to be justified, listing any known reasons against imposing such restrictions.[35] Also, any previous requests for control orders or preventative detention orders, or detention under State preventative detention laws of any kind against the suspect and their outcomes, as well as previous revocation requests must be disclosed.[36] Previous requests or orders do not preclude the individual from being issued a new iCO.[37] The final inclusions relate to a suspect's age[38] and a summary of the reasons for making the order. However, the summary is exempt from disclosing any information likely to prejudice national security, as set out in the *National Security Information (Criminal and Civil Proceedings) Act 2004* (NSIA).[39] The NSIA was set up to prevent sensitive information being disclosed in federal criminal and civil proceedings, except if this would seriously interfere with the administration of justice.[40] Individuals are not completely excluded from knowing the case against them, but information is limited due to the impact of the NSIA.

Conditional to judicial approval, the AG can grant the iCO, requesting that certain amendments be made.[41] Subject to the AG's consent, the AFP requests an

[33] 104.2 (2)—What is or is not considered a terrorist organisation in Australia is determined by the Attorney General based on intelligence, or a court might decide it is. So in determining the prerequisite for a control order to be issued on the basis of training with a terrorist organisation, the AG is involved both at the supporting the issuance of a control order, as well as the conditions giving rise to it.

[34] 104.2 (3)(a)(b).

[35] 104.2 (3)(c).

[36] 104.2 (3) (d).

[37] 104.5.

[38] iCOs cannot be sought for persons under the age of 16.

[39] 104.2 (3A).

[40] S 3(1)—the term "seriously" is not further defined in the act.

[41] 104.2 (4).

issuing court's approval,[42] providing the same documents, which are either sworn or affirmed, as well as a copy of the AG's consent.[43]

Prior to the issuing of a iCO, the court satisfies itself that the AFP followed the proper procedure outlined above, and receives and considers any further information it deems necessary to make the decision. Section 104.4(1) states that an iCO is issued if

(c) the court is satisfied on the balance of probabilities:

1. that making the order would substantially assist in preventing a terrorist act; or
2. that the person has provided training to, or received training from, a listed terrorist organisation; and

(d) the court is satisfied on the balance of probabilities that each of the obligations, prohibitions and restrictions to be imposed on the person by the order is reasonably necessary, and reasonably appropriate and adapted, for the purpose of protecting the public from a terrorist act.[44]

The court must consider the impact of the order on the individual, both financial and personal, determining if it is reasonably necessary, appropriate and adapted.[45] It is not bound by the AFP's obligations and can decide not to impose certain restrictions.[46]

An iCO must adhere to the following elements[47]:

(a) state that the court is satisfied of the matters mentioned in paragraphs 104.4(1)(c) and (d); and
(b) specify the name of the person to whom the order relates; and
(c) specify all of the obligations, prohibitions and restrictions mentioned in subsection (3) that are to be imposed on the person by the order; and
(d) state that the order does not begin to be in force until it is served personally on the person; and
(e) specify a day on which the person may attend the court for the court to:
    (1) confirm (with or without variation) the interim control order; or
    (2) declare the interim control order to be void; or
    (3) revoke the interim control order; and

---

[42] The definition of an issuing court was inserted into s.100.1(1) of the *Criminal Code 1995* by the *Anti-Terrorism* (*No. 2 Act*) *2005* and refers to (a) the Federal Court of Australia; or (b) the Family Court of Australia; or (c) the Federal Magistrates Court.

[43] 104.3.

[44] 104.4 (1).

[45] 104.4 (2).

[46] 104.4 (3).

[47] 104.5.

(f) specify the period during which the confirmed control order is to be in force, which must not end more than 12 months after the day on which the interim control order is made[48]; and
(g) state that the person's lawyer may attend a specified place in order to obtain a copy of the interim control order; and
(h) set out a summary of the grounds on which the order is made.[49]

A controlee must be served at least 48 h before the date of commencement.

3.3.1.1 Obligations

The obligations set out in s. 104.5(3) are very similar to those in the UK NDCOs, including restrictions on travel, remaining in certain locations during certain times of the day, being electronically tagged, limiting the association with certain individuals, strict communication rules, consenting to having their photograph and fingerprints taken.[50] The person may also need to participate in counselling or education programs.[51] Access to legal representation is not affected unless the person's lawyer is listed as one of the individuals with whom contact is prohibited in the obligations.

3.3.2 Appeal Process

A person subject to a cCO can apply for its revocation or variation at any point after it has been issued by outlining the reasons in writing to the AFP Commissioner.[52] As above, the AFP, the controlee and/or their representative(s) may provide further evidence or support. The AFP Commissioner can do the same, by applying to the court to either vary or remove conditions of the order, or to revoke it altogether. He must inform the controlee in writing of the application to do so and the reasons for which he is doing so. Again, the usual individuals[53] are able to provide further evidence or submissions. Any additional obligations must be justified by having reasonable grounds for believing they would aid in preventing a terrorist attack.[54] The AFP Commissioner needs to present the court with the

---

[48] The maximum duration for a 16–18 year old is 3 months (104.28(2)). s104.5(2) specifies that successive COs can be made against the same person.

[49] Subject to National Security exclusions in the NSIA 2004.

[50] For the duration of the order only—these are to be destroyed as soon as the order is no longer in effect.

[51] A person may chose not to participate in counselling or education (s104.5(6)).

[52] And the Queensland public interest monitor if applicable.

[53] 104.19 (3).

[54] 104.23(1).

justification thereof, including any known facts which might go against this imposition, along with any previous applications relating to the case. Furthermore, he also needs to provide the controlee with the same reasoning and documents. Again, the usual National Security exemptions apply, and the usual people are able to provide further evidence.

The court can either revoke a cCO, vary the conditions within, or dismiss the application made by the person in question or the AFP with immediate effect if it is satisfied that making the order would substantially assist in preventing a terrorist attack or that the person has provided or received terrorist training (104.4(1)(c)), or indeed is not satisfied that the conditions are reasonably necessary, appropriate for the purpose of protecting the public (s104.4(1)(d)). The threshold is on the balance of probabilities. The impact of any additional obligations on a person's personal and financial circumstances need to be considered by the court prior to introducing the change.[55] Any changes to or revocations of the cCO must be served to the controlee as soon as practicable and in person by a member of the AFP, taking care to ensure the information has been understood by the person in question.[56]

A controlee's lawyer can obtain a copy of the confirmed order, but is not entitled to be shown or provided copies of any other documents.[57] As with the iCO, photographs and fingerprints taken as part of the order are only used to ensure compliance with the order and must be destroyed as soon as the order ceases to be in force. Non-compliance is a punishable offence.[58]

3.4 Comparison of UK and Australian Control Orders

Having established that the Australian control order system, though based on the British model, contains some significant differences, the aim of this section is to compare and contrast the two statutory provisions. Much of the analysis employs the terminology set out in Sect. 2.5 so as to differentiate between different gradients of prevention.

The underlying purpose of both statutes is that these obligations protect the public from a terrorist attack. In essence, these obligations and restrictions are designed to affect the controlees' routine by removing the opportunities to engage in terrorism-related activity. The wording of the aim of the relevant acts reveals some interesting differences between the two approaches. For instance, the aim of the PTA 2005, *to prevent or restrict further involvement* demonstrates a clear preventive intent. However, determining whether or not it falls on the pre-emptive

---

[55] 104.24(2).

[56] 104.26(4) states that not complying with this requirement does not affect the validity of the order.

[57] 104.21.

[58] 104.22(3) Imprisonment for 2 years.

or reactive prevention side is more difficult due to the wording that precedes it. Control orders were made against *individuals involved in terrorism-related activity*, bypassing suspicion/allegation, apparently having determined their prior involvement. Indeed, the *further involvement* would support this assumption. This would indicate that British control orders were reactively preventive. However, in NDCO cases, the Home Secretary only needed reasonable grounds for suspecting involvement, swinging the pendulum back towards a more pre-emptive focus. Indeed, the lower burden of proof and lack of sufficient evidence to prosecute any such alleged involvement creates an interesting juxtaposition between the statutory wording and the practical application of UK control orders, which will be further explored in Sect. 4.3.

In comparison, the Australian statute requires the senior AFP member to have reasonable grounds either that the order *would substantially assist in preventing a terrorist act* or that the individual in question *has provided training to, or received training from, a listed terrorist organisation.* The first condition implies that the involvement in terrorist-related activity is but a mere suspicion at that point in time, since more certain allegations would be expected to result in prosecution under one of the many new anti-terrorism laws. Thus, if issued on the first premise alone, it would be true to state that it would fall under pre-emptive prevention. The second requirement, however, implies some form of past conduct, making it reactively preventive. In this sense, Australian control orders may not necessarily be pre-emptive measures at all.

The role of the police in requesting control orders also differs between jurisdictions. In the UK, the police were meant to be consulted throughout about whether or not sufficient evidence existed to prosecute an individual. Moreover, continual monitoring was in place to gather evidence in support of prosecution, which appears to be a rather futile exercise when the individual is under the kind of strict obligations specifically designed to prevent the controlee from engaging in further conduct. The actual control order, however, was requested by the Home Secretary. The AFP plays a much more active part in determining against whom they wish to issue an iCO, although the Attorney-General's consent is required prior to the application being put before the courts. The Australian statute provides for a potentially more objective/balanced portrayal of reasons to issue a control order, considering counter-arguments are also required. Whether or not this is implemented in practice is a different matter, and is examined further in the next chapter. Also, this does not mean the British Home Secretary might not have included such considerations, even if not required to do so according to the statute. Both the UK and Australia decided to set the burden of proof for seeking a control order to *on reasonable grounds*.

The power to decide whether or not to issue an order ultimately lies with the Judiciary. Court proceedings again vary by jurisdiction. Both systems have a preliminary/interim and confirmation hearing, however the Australian control order changes status once confirmed. The burden of proof for NDCOs in British courts remained unaltered; their Australian counterparts, however, require judges to be satisfied *on the balance of probabilities*.

Whereas the UK's procedures were generally *ex parte*, the Australian two-tiered approach of interim and confirmed orders allows for the person in question, or controlee, to either be present and/or represented at the confirmation hearing. Moreover, they are provided with a summary of the grounds for issuance, and the opportunity to provide evidence in their defence, something controlees before British judges were not privy to.

Because of the PTA forerunner's association with immigration law, control order proceedings in the UK appropriated certain practices from the SIAC hearings. Closed hearings and Special Advocates were used in an effort to address some of the procedural shortcomings associated with national security concerns. Similar concerns are circumvented in Australia, the *National Security Information (Criminal and Civil Proceedings) Act 2004* ensuring restrictions on disclosing sensitive evidence or intelligence to both the controlee and/or the general public are upheld.

Given the controversial nature of the control order regime, human rights concerns were bound to come up, especially given its forerunner's record. Different concerns arose within the two jurisdictions, chiefly relating to the length of the curfew and the interpretation of house arrest. However, the UK introduced its own Human Rights Act in 1998, and is subject to the European Convention of Human Rights (ECHR). Australia has no Bill of Rights at the Commonwealth level, instead relying on the Constitution for guidance in such matters.[59] This lack of an additional oversight mechanism has drawn heavy criticism, despite Australia being a signatory to the International Covenant on Civil and Political Rights (ICCPR) (International Commission of Jurists 2009; Jaggers 2008; Michaelsen 2005).

The person in question was notified of the control order against him or her only after it was approved by the UK court. In Australia, the iCO only comes into force once personally served on them by a member of the AFP.

A final point to highlight is the statutory grounds for the court refusing to issue a control order. In Australia, if the court disagrees that one or both of the necessary prerequisite conditions applies, or it believes the conditions are not reasonably necessary or adapted to achieve the aim, it can refuse issuance. In the UK, if the court found that the Home Secretary's decision to make the control order was obviously flawed, it was obliged to quash the order. The same principle applied to flawed obligations. Modifications of the sometimes very restrictive obligations

---

[59] The terrorism debate has to some extent accelerated the debate whether or not Australia needs a Bill of Rights, see for instance Williams (2004) and Saul (2007) for a more general account of administrative law on human rights.

were permitted and were able to be instigated at the controlee or Home Secretary's request in the UK. In Australia, the same applies, however judges may make alterations a condition for approval.

While the British control order provisions incorporated a more judicial approach compared to previous executive measures (Walker 2011), they did not provide the same oversight or indeed procedural safeguards as the Australian regime. The use of closed hearings and Special Advocates has laid the foundations for anti-terrorism cases being turned into inquisitorial tribunals. Indeed, Bonner (2007) argued that SIAC might eventually turn into a court specialising in national security issues. While no derogating control orders have been issued, thus technically not depriving individuals of their liberty, important concerns have nonetheless been raised. In total, 52 individuals were subjected to a non-derogating control order in the UK, compared to only two in Australia. It is to the application of the above statutes I now turn.

References

Bonner, D. (2006). Checking the executive? Detention without trial, control orders, due process and human rights. *European Public Law,12*(1), 45–71.

Bonner, D. (2007). *Executive measures, terrorism and national security: Have the rules of the game changed?* Aldershot: Ashgate.

International Commission of Jurists. (2009). Assessing damage, urging action: Report of the eminent jurists panel on terrorism, counter-terrorism and human rights. In I. C. o. Jurists (Ed.). Geneva: International Commission of Jurists.

Ip, J. (2007). Comparative perspectives on the detention of terrorist suspects. *Transnational Law and Contemporary Problems,16*, 773–871.

Jaggers, B. (2008). *Anti-terrorism control orders in Australia and the United Kingdom: A comparison*. Canberra: Parliamentary Library, Department of Parliamentary Services.

McDonald, G. (2007). Control orders and preventative detention—why alarm is misguided. In A. Lynch, E. MacDonald, & G. Williams (Eds.), *Law and liberty in the war on terror*. Sydney: Federation Press.

Michaelsen, C. (2005). International human rights on trial-the United Kingdom's and Australia's legal response to 9/11. *Sydney Law Review,25*(3), 275–303.

Saul, B. (2007). Australian administrative law: The human rights dimension. In M. Groves & H. P. Lee (Eds.), *Australian administrative law: Fundamentals, principles and doctrines*. Cambridge: Cambride University Press.

Shah, S. (2005). The UK's anti-terror legislation and the house of lords: The first skirmish. *Human Rights Law Review,5*(2), 403–421. doi:10.1093/hrlr/ngi025.

Smith, A. T. H. (2007). Balancing liberty and security? A legal analysis of United Kingdom anti-terrorist legislation. *European Journal on Criminal Policy Research, 13*, 73–83 (Fear v. Freedom Post 9/11 - the European Perspective).

Walker, C. (2011). *Terrorism and the law*. Oxford: Oxford University Press.

Williams, G. (2004). *The case for an Australian bill of rights: Freedom in the war on terror*. Sydney: UNSW Press.

Chapter 4
Comparing Control Order Implementations

4.1 Introduction

The statutory analysis of the control order regimes highlighted important distinctions between how the two countries incorporated the restriction of opportunities to engage in terrorism-related activity into the legal framework. While the British provisions are more executive-driven, their Australian counterparts provide for greater judicial input. Moreover, the Australian statute incorporates both a reactively preventive and pre-emptive rationale. It is perhaps not surprising then that the differences in approach are also reflected in the practical application of the control order scheme. Probably the most obvious difference is the number of control orders issued. Given that there have only been two Australian control order cases, this chapter begins with an examination of the legal issues arising from Jack Thomas and David Hicks' control orders. Due to the number of British cases, a summary of the legal challenges illustrates the principal tests to the scheme.

4.2 Australian Control Order Cases

4.2.1 The Jack Thomas Case

Joseph "Jack" Thomas was originally acquitted of two counts of providing support to a terrorist organization, but found guilty of intentionally receiving funds from a terrorist organization and being in possession of a falsified Australian passport by a Victorian Supreme Court in February 2006.[1] Apparently unaware he had done anything wrong, Thomas made self-inculpatory statements during an interview with Australian Federal Police (AFP) officers in Pakistan in March 2003, which

[1] *DPP (Cth) v Thomas* (Sentence) [2006] VSC 120 (31 March 2006). See Lynch (2006) for a more detailed analysis of the issues raised in that case.

S. Donkin, *Preventing Terrorism and Controlling Risk*, Springer Briefs in International and Comparative Criminology, DOI: 10.1007/978-1-4614-8705-0_4,

were later relied upon as evidence by the prosecution. Thomas appealed on the grounds that the interview evidence should not have been admissible. On August 18, 2006 his ground for appeal was upheld and his two convictions quashed.[2] However, less than ten days later, control order proceedings commenced.

On August 27, 2006, the Federal Magistrates Court of Australia in Canberra ordered Australia's first interim control order to be issued against Jack Thomas.[3] The order set out that the AFP Manager of Domestic Terrorism, Ramzi Jabbour, had applied for the order to be made in accordance with s104.4. After considering the information, the court stated it was satisfied on the balance of probabilities that the order would substantially assist in the prevention of a terrorist attack, and that Thomas had received training from a listed terrorist organizations. Furthermore, it was satisfied on the balance of probabilities that each obligation was reasonably necessary, appropriate and adapted to protect the public.

The obligations, prohibitions and restrictions imposed under the iCO[4] were that Thomas:

- remain at his home between midnight and 5 a.m. each day[5];
- report to one of three named Victoria Police Stations, three times a week on specific days within a 12 h window[6];
- have his fingerprints taken within 24 h of the iCO being issued, and, if requested, during the above reporting duties;
- not leave the country without written AFP consent;
- have nothing to do with explosives, weapons and combat skills, whether in document form (incl. electronic copies), physically or by communication; especially communicating his knowledge to individuals known to belong to an organization on the list of terrorist organizations, as well as not passing on the names and details of individuals known to be associated;
- not communicate or associate with specifically listed/named individuals, or anyone he knows to be a member of a listed terrorist organization[7];
- limit the following communication devices to one AFP approved service/device within 48 h of the iCO being served:
  - mobile phone, phone card, SIM card or account, landline phone service, VOIP service,[8] internet service provider and e-mail account;

[2] *R v Thomas* (2006) 14 VR 475.

[3] *Jabbour v Thomas* [2006] FMCA 1286.

[4] Contained in Schedule 1 of the iCO.

[5] Unless the AFP is notified in advance of a different address.

[6] Unless otherwise agreed in writing with the AFP.

[7] Schedule 3 contains a list of terrorist organizations, listed people were determined by the Department of Foreign Affairs and Trade.

[8] Voice over internet protocol, e.g. Skype.

- have no access to satellite phones or public telephones[9];
- surrender all firearms and ammunition to police within 48 h of the iCO being served.

In February 2007, Thomas sought to quash his iCO arguing that Division 104 of the *Criminal Code 1995* (Cth) was invalid.[10] He made several constitutional challenges to the validity of the control order regime, including that it confers non-judicial power on a federal court, it was not supported by one or more express or implied heads of legislative power under the Constitution, and the judicial power conferred by Division 104 was exercised contrary to constitutional provisions. In a majority ruling, the High Court ruled that interim control orders were constitutional.

The Thomas case reveals the inherent complexity of pre-emption and its application within the traditional legal framework. The principal points of contention weave a rich tapestry of legal doctrines dating back decades, even centuries. This case was the first, and thus far, only case to challenge the Australian anti-terrorism control order regime. Of interest to this research are the issues relating to the separation of powers and the sanctioning of anticipated conduct. As Lynch has commented, the case examined the role of the Judiciary in response to executive decisions made in light of the threat of terrorism, i.e. whether it upholds the traditional review function or whether it becomes an active participant in developing feasible procedures of preventive justice (Lynch 2008).

Thomas argued that the Judiciary is usually called upon to adjudicate reactively on past infractions; any pre-emptive action is the domain of the Executive. Although Thomas tried to argue that the overarching aim of protecting the public is one only the Executive can consider, it was found to be consistent with judicial functions. As Lynch (2008) pointed out, it is important to examine this question in the context of executive detention of aliens or state courts issuing preventive detention of dangerous offenders. He succinctly clarified the question as "whether a federal court (as opposed to a state court or the Commonwealth Executive) could deprive a citizen (as opposed to an alien) of their liberty, stopping short of full detention, absent any earlier finding of criminal guilt whatsoever" (Lynch 2008, p. 1201). The Commonwealth of Australia argued that anti-terrorism laws with the aim of protecting the public from an attack should be recognized as an additional exception (Bennett 2007).

As for ruling on the past, Hayne J's dissenting opinion highlighted that the traditional adversarial system was concerned with adjudicating differing views of past events. Since the iCO hearing is ex parte, this process is undermined, as the person in question is unable to contest the evidence presented against him. The role of a judge, certainly in the interim hearing, thus acquires a more inquisitorial role, examining the evidence presented by the police. Hayne J also questioned the

---

[9] A public telephone could be used in an emergency.

[10] *Thomas v Mowbray* [2007] HCA 33.

role and reliability of the intelligence material presented, as it did not stand up to the traditional standards of evidence. In cases where courts are required to take future conduct into consideration, Hayne J argued that such decisions were usually supported by expert evidence, again of a higher and more rigorous nature than the intelligence relied upon in terrorist cases. Accepting intelligence material as substantially correct and subsequently issuing control orders on the basis of the credibility of the senior AFP agent making the case exemplifies Hayne J's concerns about undermining institutional impartiality. However, it has to be said that Mowbray FM did exercise judicial discretion with regard to the obligations sought in the original iCO. Rather than accepting Jabbour's proposed obligations without question, Mowbray modified the obligations, removing the controversial provision for religious and psychological counselling, as well as the originally rather excessive list of people whom Thomas was prohibited from contacting. Thus, the Federal Magistrate exercised his judicial discretion during the interim hearing, ensuring judicial oversight of the control order scheme.

Despite Hayne and Kirby JJ's dissent, Thomas' arguments relating to the incompatibility with federal judicial power, such as the ex parte nature of the iCO, the threshold of burden of proof, and the court enforcing its own orders were dismissed as not constituting novel proceedings, since examples of each already existed outside of the terrorism context.[11] References to historical antecedents abound, their applicability and parallels to control orders were contested among the High Court judges. The *Fardon* case[12] was cited as upholding the power to make interim detention orders against currently imprisoned sex offenders considered dangerous. As previously highlighted, interim detention orders against convicted offenders are examples of reactive prevention, and thus present different considerations to making similar orders on anticipated as opposed to past actions. Indeed, in *Fardon* the High Court was unable to answer whether pre-emptive detention is in fact judicial in nature (Lynch 2008).

As for the determination of guilt, control orders, being civil in nature, do not require a finding of guilt. In the High Court, the majority found that since the orders neither involved punishment nor were intended to be punitive, Thomas' arguments relating to the Judiciary imposing detention without a finding of guilt should be dismissed. The notion of imposing restrictions on the basis of past or anticipated conduct is central to the issuance of control orders, not least due to the wording of the grounds for issuance. As discussed in the previous chapter, Australian control orders can be issued if one or both of the necessary conditions, i.e. assisting in the prevention of an attack or the person has trained with a listed organisation, are fulfilled. In Thomas' case, Mowbray FM, admitting the contested interview evidence of having trained with Al-Qaeda and Jabbour's confirmation

---

[11] An example of an ex parte hearing are apprehended violence orders. *Nicholas v R* (1998) 193 CLR 173 established that Parliament can alter rules of both evidence and procedure, including the burden of proof without violating Chapter III (Bennett).

[12] *Fardon v Attorney-General (Qld)* (2004) 223 CLR 575.

thereof, made it clear that the second condition had been fulfilled[13]; this evidence also formed the basis for his assumption that Thomas might pose a danger in the future, thus satisfying the first condition of potential anticipated future offending. Would the pre-emptive first requirement be met without the reactive second requirement? I recall Kirby J's finding that the second element is not a necessary pre-requisite for issuance. A jury with access to the same information (evidence) acquitted him in the criminal trial with a higher burden of proof; yet it is considered sufficient in a civil trial with a lower threshold (Lynch 2008). However, Thomas was not charged with receiving training from a listed organisation, an offence under s.102.5 of the *Criminal Code* (*Cth*). The inadmissibility of the controversial AFP interview may have determined the decision not to prosecute on that charge. The lower level of proof in the civil control order procedure, however, may have provided the ideal platform for the AFP to react to an offence which was not prosecutable in a criminal court, in which case, his control order would most definitely constitute an example of reactive prevention. On the other hand, Thomas may not have been able to be charged with the s 102.5 offence, as he allegedly trained with Al-Qaeda prior to the law's existence, pre 9/11. One might argue then, that Thomas' control order was not just reactively preventive, but an attempt at retrospectively sanctioning behaviour currently defined as criminal.

As for the outcome of the Thomas case, in December 2006, the Court of Appeal ordered a re-trial on the two counts for which he was first convicted based on an interview given to the Australian Broadcasting Company (ABC). In August 2007 a majority ruling of 5:2 in the High Court determined that issuing control orders, as provided for in Subdivision B, is indeed valid and rejected his appeal. At this point, Thomas' iCO was still in place and unconfirmed, eleven months after it was issued. Since his re-trial at the Supreme Court was not set to commence until February 2008, Thomas agreed to follow similar obligations to those in his iCO until the trial's conclusion. In return, the AFP agreed not seek another control order. Thomas was eventually cleared of all terrorism-related charges, but found guilty of falsifying his passport on October 23, 2008.[14]

4.2.2 The David Hicks Case

Safe in the knowledge that the Australian control order system was not unconstitutional, a second control order was ordered sixteen months after Thomas' iCO, this time against an Australian returning from Guantanamo Bay. David Matthew Hicks is an Australian who was sent to Guantanamo Bay after being captured in Afghanistan and sold to US Special Forces by the Northern Alliance in December

---

[13] A point contested by Hayne J, who argued that despite Thomas' admission, this was not an established fact.

[14] *R v Thomas (No 4)* [2008] VSCA 107.

2001. He was held in Guantanamo between January 2002 and 2007. Hicks' detention by the US predated the Howard Government's anti-terrorism legislation, meaning that if Hicks had been returned to Australia at that point, he could not have been prosecuted for any offences (Australian Associated Press 2007; Lasry 2007).

Hicks' case was eventually brought before the newly created Military Commission[15] at Guantanamo in August 2004, where he was charged with conspiracy, murder and aiding the enemy. However, his trial was delayed after the Military Commission was found to be unconstitutional and in violation of international law.[16] After President Bush ensured the constitutionality of the Military Commission with the introduction of a new act,[17] Hicks was eventually charged with a new, retrospective offence, providing material support to terrorism, to which he pleaded guilty as part of a plea bargain, receiving a seven year sentence (having already spent six years and three months in prison). He was eventually returned to Australia in May 2007, where he served out the remainder of his sentence in Yatala Prison in Adelaide.[18]

Hicks (2010) has since stated that he did not train with Al-Qaeda or any other terrorist group; nor did he engage in or plan any acts of terrorism during his time abroad. He also denied ever having confessed to supporting terrorism (Hicks 2010).

4.2.2.1 The Interim Control Order

On December 21, 2007 the Federal Magistrates Court of Australia approved an iCO be issued against David Hicks. After considering the information supplied by the AFP the court stated it was satisfied on the balance of probabilities that the order would substantially assist in the prevention of a terrorist attack, and that Hicks had received training from a listed terrorist organization. Furthermore, it was satisfied on the balance of probabilities that each obligation was reasonably necessary, appropriate and adapted to protect the public. Indeed, the majority of conditions in the iCO were almost identical to that issued against Thomas.[19] However, one important difference emerged, namely that Hicks was, at the time of issuance, in custody in Yatala Prison and the obligations would only come into force upon his release.

The obligations, prohibitions and restrictions imposed under Hicks' iCO[20] were for him to:

---

[15] A departure from the usual US military judicial system.

[16] *Hamdan v Rumsfeld* 548 US 557 (2006).

[17] Military Commissions Act 2006 (US).

[18] For a detailed summary review of the decisions leading up to the control order, see Lasry (2007).

[19] There was no mention of the summary of grounds on which the order was made, but it was included in Schedule 2.

[20] Contained in Schedule 1 of the iCO.

- remain at a specified address between midnight and 6 a.m. each day[21];
- report to a member of South Australia (SA) Police, three times a week on specific days within a 16 h window[22];
- have his fingerprints taken within 24 h of his release from prison, and, if requested, during the above reporting duties;
- not leave the country without written AFP consent;
- have nothing to do with explosives, weapons, combat skills or military tactics, whether in document form (incl. electronic copies), physically or by communication; especially communicating his knowledge to individuals known to belong to an organization on the list of terrorist organizations, as well as not passing on the names and details of individuals known to be associated;
- not communicate or associate with anyone he knows to be a member of a listed terrorist organization[23];
- limit the following communication devices to one AFP approved service/devices:
  - mobile phone, phone card, SIM card or account, landline phone service, VOIP service, internet service provider and e-mail account;
- have no access to satellite phones or public telephones[24];
- surrender all firearms and ammunition; commercial, military, homemade or improvised explosive devices or accessories immediately.

The reasons for issuing the iCO for David Hicks were grounded in his having trained with two listed terrorist organizations[25] over an approximately twelve month period in 2000/2001 in Pakistan and Afghanistan. This knowledge allegedly provides both him and others with the ability to carry out a terrorist attack, as well as potentially serving as a source for other extremists. The iCO stated that the obligations set out in the control order were conceived to protect the public, reintegrate Hicks into Australian society and culture, protect him from being manipulated, and prevent his knowledge from helping others to commit terrorist acts.

4.2.2.2 Summary

David Hicks' case contributes several interesting facts in the examination of preemption. Firstly, his control order was issued to coincide with his release from prison. Ignoring the debate about whether or not he should have been incarcerated in Australia after his release from Guantanamo, Hicks served the full sentence

---

[21] With provision to request an amendment to the address for specific reasons from the AFP.

[22] Unless otherwise agreed in writing with the AFP.

[23] Schedule 3 contains a list of terrorist organizations, listed people were determined by the Department of Foreign Affairs and Trade.

[24] A public telephone could be used in an emergency.

[25] Lashkar-e-Tayyiba (LeT) and Al Qaída.

imposed by the US Military Commission. The issuing of a control order upon his release can therefore not be considered as a condition for early release or parole of any kind. Indeed, Federal Magistrate Donald said as much when declaring it a prospective protection of the public.

As for the issuing procedure, although ex parte, Hicks' legal representatives were present at the interim hearing. More importantly, as with Thomas, the magistrate exercised his judicial discretion to amend the AFP-suggested obligations to better suit the controlee. Although the reduction in the reporting requirement was initiated by Hicks' legal team, the reduction in the curfew hours and the residential extension to the whole of Australia originated with Donald FM.

Hicks' personal account provides valuable, albeit subjective insight into how the control order affected his life. Since the AFP were unable to provide him with or approve access to a computer which he was entitled to under the control order, a restriction essentially became a deprivation. It would appear that the control order lived up to its name, exerting control over his actions and his life. Despite the relatively short curfew requirement, in combination with the other obligations Hicks felt he was still in custody. In this sense, control orders, although non-punitive in theory, appear to evoke a sense of punishment and detention in those subject to them.

4.3 UK Control Order Application

4.3.1 Legal Challenges

Control orders originated with the Executive. However, there were two inbuilt safeguards in the control order regime, judicial review and the necessity for annual renewal based on the Independent Reviewer of Terrorism's annual reports and recommendations (Bonner 2006). The aim of the following section is to provide a brief overview of some of the most pertinent and influential court challenges arising in response to the scheme. Given the greater number of orders issued in the UK compared to Australia, a thorough examination of each case akin to the one conducted above was beyond the scope of this study. Moreover, given the secret nature of many proceedings, this undertaking would have been nigh impossible.

Given that control orders originated in reaction to a legal challenge of their predecessor, the ACTSA, it is perhaps not surprising that the new measure was also subject to legal scrutiny, especially given its implications for the legal process. The Belmarsh case[26] has contributed to executive measures being increasingly scrutinised by the courts, as has the legislation itself, by encouraging judicial review (Walker 2011). In relation to control orders, judicial involvement has been controversial due to the anticipatory risk assessment they are asked to undertake

---

[26] *A and others v Secretary of State for the Home Department* [2004] UKHL 56.

(Walker 2011). Much in the same way this issue was debated in the Australian context in the Thomas case, critics considered this external to the judicial role, seemingly neglecting to acknowledge that this is precisely what judges are asked to consider on a daily basis when making bail or sentencing decisions (Walker 2011). Since their introduction in 2005, several individuals subject to non-derogating control orders launched legal challenges in response to their control order. The majority of appeals centred around the obligations set out in the orders (Jaggers 2008), many of which related to the length of the curfew imposed and whether it constituted a breach under Article 5 of the ECHR (deprivation of liberty). Probably the most influential case pertaining to acceptable curfew duration is *JJ*, which set the precedent for an upper limit of 16 h. The second theme to emerge is the concern surrounding an individual's right to receive a fair trial in line with Article 6, secret evidence and Special Advocates proving especially contentious. The two key trials with regard to procedural issues are *MB* and *AF*.[27] Although both individuals were suspected of having links to extremists, the material at the heart of the justification for the control orders was contained in the secret information. Given the civil nature of the control order process, the House of Lords found that the Home Secretary need not refer to a specific offence given that the aim of the order was preventive in nature and not punitive or retributive (Walker 2011).

The PTA 2005 clearly distinguishes between two distinct species of control order. To date, Britain has only issued the non-derogating variety, meaning no derogation from Article 5 of the ECHR was necessary. In practice, however, the duration some controlees were required to remain at a specified address was initially up to 18 h.[28] In *Secretary of State for the Home Department v JJ and others (FC)*[29] the Court of Appeal found that the 18 h curfew, being electronically tagged, being subjected to random searches, as well as restrictions on movement within a specified radius, twice daily reporting requirements, as well as prohibitions on who they could meet and how they could communicate,[30] amounted to a breach of Article 5, i.e. a deprivation of liberty, and could therefore not be made by the Home Secretary alone (International Commission of Jurists 2009; Ip 2007; Macdonald 2007; Walker 2011). The House of Lords upheld the decision, finding that the cumulative effect of these obligations and restrictions was incompatible with Article 5 and amounted to conditions resembling solitary confinement for an indefinite duration. Although the analogy of an open prison was put forward by the Law Lords, they found controlees to be at a greater disadvantage due to the restrictions on contact or indeed entertainment (Walker 2011). Moreover, some controlees had been relocated to unfamiliar areas, thus depriving them of familiar

---

[27] [2007] UKHL 46 and [2009] UKHL 28 respectively.

[28] The average curfew length between 2006 and 2011 was 12.1 h in the UK, compared to the Australian average of 4.5 h.

[29] [2007] UKHL 45.

[30] Other obligations included limited (pre-approved) visitors, being subjected to searches, and no mobile phone or internet communication.

social contacts. It was held that their lives were wholly regulated by the Home Office. Lord Bingham[31] found that "[b]ecause account must be taken of an individual's whole situation it seems to me inappropriate to draw a sharp distinction between a period of confinement which will, and one which will not, amount to a deprivation of liberty, important though the period of daily confinement will be in any overall assessment." That being said, Lord Brown proffered 16 h as being the upper limit of curfews, but still acknowledged that it might be excessive. Indeed, in the case of *E*, a 12 h curfew and other obligations were not considered a deprivation of liberty. Not even the 14 h issued to MB or AF qualified as a deprivation of liberty. It would appear that despite the reluctance of some to specify an accepted threshold, this is precisely what has emerged.

In this regard, the case of *Secretary of the State for the Home Department v MB* held that there was no determination of a criminal charge or any particular criminal offence in NDCO cases, and no assertion of criminal conduct; it was based on suspicion alone. Moreover, the purpose of the order was identified as being preventive, not punitive or retributive. The same was held in *AF*:

> Prevention is one of the recognised aims and consequences of punishment and the effect of a preventative measure may be so adverse as to be penal in its effects if not in its intention.
>
> I would on balance accept the Secretary of State's submission that non-derogating control order proceedings do not involve the determination of a criminal charge. Parliament has gone to some lengths to avoid a procedure which crosses the criminal boundary: there is no assertion of criminal conduct, only a foundation of suspicion; no identification of any specific criminal offence is provided for; the order made is preventative in purpose, not punitive or retributive; and the obligations imposed must be no more restrictive than are judged necessary to achieve the preventative object of the order.
>
> *Lord Bingham of Cornhill at 23 and 24*

Lord Hoffmann further elaborated on the pre-emptive intention underlying the control order scheme (at 48 in *AF*):

> The order is made on the basis of suspicion about what they may do in the future and not upon a determination of what they have done in the past. And the restrictions imposed by the order are for the purpose of prevention and not punishment or deterrence.

There was no restriction beyond what was considered necessary to be preventative. ECHR Article 6(1) entitles the controlee to a level of procedural protection commensurate with the gravity of the potential consequences, especially if the order might contain stringent obligations. It applies to both civil and criminal cases, but justifies certain constraints in the interest of national security and justice.

The third issue in *MB* was determining whether or not the Home Secretary's reasons to impose the control order were flawed. Originally, the High Court found that the procedure of imposing NDCOs was in violation of Article 6 of the ECHR, due to the Home Secretary's reasoning being flawed on the grounds of information available at the time of issuance only, thus weakening any judicial supervision.[32]

---

[31] Ibid, at 16.

[32] In accordance with section 3(10) of the *PTA 2005*.

However, this finding was later overturned by the Court of Appeal[33] which found that all information available at the time of the court hearing needed to be taken into account (Ip 2007). Indeed, the case divided judicial opinion, ranging from Lord Hoffmann dissenting on the grounds that Special Advocates provided sufficient protection to ensure a fair trial, to Lord Bingham who asserted that the use of closed material could never ensure the "irreducible minimum of procedural protection" guaranteed by Article 6 (Kavanagh 2010).[34]

Indeed, a Constitutional Affairs Committee Report (2005) had already identified "a number of defects with the Special Advocate system" even prior to its application in conjunction with the PTA (p. 3). It proposed several amendments to improve the fairness of the system and the communication between the appellants and the Special Advocates (Constitutional Affairs Committee 2005). The role of Special Advocates was further explored in the case of *AF*. At issue was whether the presence of Special Advocates sufficiently compensated for the non-adversarial hearing to still be compatible with Article 6 requirements of a fair trial. The House of Lords found that in cases where the case against a controlee was heavily based on secret evidence, the right to a fair trial was indeed compromised (Kavanagh 2010).

> I agree further that the special advocate procedure, highly likely though it is that it will in fact safeguard the suspect against significant injustice, cannot invariably be guaranteed to do so.
>
> *Lord Brown, at 90*

The Home Secretary's case against MB included both open and secret material, but the justification for imposing the order was contained in the closed material.[35] After the Appeal Court judgment in *MB*, the court was required to decide whether the information upon which the Home Secretary relied actually amounted to reasonable grounds for suspecting involvement in terrorist activity, as well as deciding upon the necessity of each of the requested obligations. The Cerie Bullivant[36] case further clarified several issues relating to the disclosure of evidence and the role of Special Advocates. Material should only be withheld if its disclosure would obviously be detrimental to the public interest. As for the Special Advocates, it was held that they could communicate with the individual to identify matters which would help support the defence. Ordering disclosure on the grounds of fairness alone prior to the testing of evidence will only be ordered in exceptional circumstances. If at the end of the hearing the court finds a breach of Article 6, it must give the Home Secretary the opportunity to disclose further evidence so as to remedy the potential breach.

---

33 [2006] EWCA (Civ) 1140.

34 See Kavanagh for an in-depth analysis of the MB and AF cases and their compatibility with the HRA.

35 *Secretary of State for the Home Department (Respondent) v AF (Appellant) (FC) and another (Appellant) and one other action* [2009] UKHL 28 at 8.

36 Known initially only as AG; [2008] EWHC B2 (29 Jan 2008).

In February 2009, the Council of Europe ECHR in *A and Others v UK*[37] ruled on the issues of the effects of non-disclosure in terms of both impact on the adversarial trial procedure in the interests of national security and its effect on the right to a fair trial. It held that the interests of national security are capable of justifying the withholding of certain evidence. Nevertheless, it did acknowledge that a fair trial could only occur if the difficulties faced by the defendant's limited rights were counterbalanced by judicial procedures.[38]

> Thus, while the right to a fair criminal trial under Article 6 includes a right to disclosure of all material evidence in the possession of the prosecution, both for and against the accused, the Court has held that it might sometimes be necessary to withhold certain evidence from the defence on public interest grounds.
>
> *A and Others v United Kingdom* at 206

However, the Council did find that, in cases where the Home Secretary's case rested predominantly on secret evidence that had not been disclosed to the person in question, the Special Advocate provisions were insufficient protection given that the evidence could not be effectively challenged by the applicant.[39] As a result of the ECHR decision, Lord Phillips in *Secretary of State for the Home Department (Respondent) v AF (Appellant) (FC) and another (Appellant) and one other action*[40] acknowledged that a controlee "must be given sufficient information about the allegations against him to enable him to give effective instructions in relation to those allegations", even in the event that sources are not disclosed.[41] If, on the other hand, the case against the controlee hinges on closed materials, the requirement for a fair trial would not be satisfied.

4.4 Cross-Jurisdictional Analysis

The principal issues to arise in British legal challenges to the control order scheme were the maximum length of the curfew permitted without amounting to a deprivation of liberty; the extent to which the preventive aim resembled punishment; and the procedural fairness of the process. The case of *AF* has shown the ability of the Judiciary to be creative in its interpretation of human rights provisions, ensuring a greater compliance with procedural justice (Kavanagh 2010). Indeed, even with the increased awareness of the case against a controlee post *AF*, implementing such changes proved more difficult to do in practice, especially considering communication between the parties is still prohibited. Kavanagh

37 *A and Others v United Kingdom*, ECHR (19 February 2009).

38 Ibid at 205.

39 Ibid at 220.

40 *Secretary of State for the Home Department (Respondent) v AF (Appellant) (FC) and another (Appellant) and one other action* [2009] UKHL 28.

41 Ibid, at 59.

(2010) highlighted that the finding in *AF* may have had a significant knock-on effect on the sustainability of the control order system due to the Home Office reliance on sensitive intelligence. Moreover, it has enhanced the measures of procedural fairness, and strengthened position of Special Advocates, forcing the government to revoke orders where it is not prepared to disclose the intelligence against the controlee (Kavanagh 2010). As a result, if a judge deemed further disclosure of evidence necessary to enable the controlee to mount a more viable defence and ensure sufficient procedural protection, the Home Secretary had to decide whether to disclose further evidence, or to withdraw it all together. The Home Office faced a dilemma of disclosing sensitive information in the hope of securing a control order but potentially compromising aspects of national security, or take the risk that less sensitive information was sufficiently compelling to warrant a control order (Walker 2011). As a result, several control orders were revoked.

Although the former Independent Reviewer of Terrorism Legislation Lord Carlile reiterated his support for the control order regime throughout the years, he did at times express reservations about the extent of some of the obligations made (Carlile of Berriew 2006; Macdonald 2007). For instance, he acknowledged the arduous and severely restricting conditions some of the controlees were subject to, without having been found guilty of an offence, many of whom on suspicion alone. Even NDCOs may thus not have been proportionate due to the severe restrictions they place on individuals (Bonner 2006).

Walker described the legal challenges as having "applied an 'intense' and sustained level of judicial vigilance and regular defeats for the government" (Walker 2011, p. 323). He argued that if the system as a whole remained intact, the courts are likely to continue their challenge, ensuring more lives are improved in the process. While several authors have acknowledged the increased judicial influence on the executive measure, control orders did not adhere to criminal standards due to the fact that appeal procedures were administrative and not criminal hearings. Although the original order was civil in nature, 14 breaches were prosecuted, meaning over a quarter of all control order cases ended up turning criminal, although sentences were certainly not excessive.[42] Zedner (2007) drew attention to some controlees' conditions being loosely worded, and apparently not viable, making potential breaches more likely. That being said, control orders were intended to be limited to one year, although the option of extension existed. However, some controlees were subject to stringent restrictions for several years, exceeding a sentence for a minor offence. This was justified as being necessary to disrupt terrorist networks and instil distrust in a controlee wishing to resume activities.

In Australia, although there have only been two control orders to date, both cases provide valuable insight into the rationale for issuance, as well as its

[42] There were only two convictions for breaching a control order, resulting in sentences of 20 weeks and 15 months (Anderson 2012).

implementation. In Jack Thomas' case, the iCO, intended to be in force for a minimal amount of time, was never actually confirmed due to his challenge first of the issuing court, then the regime as a whole. David Hicks case, on the other hand, perfectly illustrates the control order process from start to finish.

Both Thomas and Hicks had allegedly participated in training with proscribed organisations prior to 9/11. However, these groups were proscribed only after the alleged training had taken place, leaving the government with no legal recourse to prosecute retrospectively. Containing both a pre-emptive and reactive condition for issuance, both control orders were justified on the basis that Thomas and Hicks had trained with proscribed organisations. The reactive element makes up one of the two conditions for issuing a control order, and in both cases, this condition has been relied upon to justify the first, and thus as grounds to issue the control order. So although it might not be a prerequisite, the reactive element has served as the foundation for both Australian cases.[43] In light of these cases, Australian control order implementations stand firmly in the reactive prevention category, therefore invalidating accounts of them being described as pre-emptive. While it is true to state that the control order aims to prevent future behaviour in a bid to protect the public, its issuance was based on past conduct. However, Lynch (2008) highlighted that while judicial work has both predictive and protective elements to it, control orders cannot be compared to other preventive orders currently in use because they extend to individuals who have not been convicted of any previous crimes. That being said, much of the discussion about anticipated conduct in *Thomas v Mowbray*, especially the historical tracing of previous measures, focused on measures which deprive individuals of their liberty. Control orders, certainly in Australia, don't go that far, their effects being limited to restrictions on liberty and requirements to report to police.

Despite arguments that the Australian control order regime is not equipped with the same legal safeguards and standards as the United Kingdom against which to challenge the regime due to its lack of a bill of rights, as well as having fewer avenues for independent oversight (Jaggers 2008), the judicial independence exercised in both cases so far indicates that this role is being fulfilled by the courts. That is, it is evident that judicial discretion was exercised by the federal magistrates in each case; in addition, the High Court has performed an appellate function.

Having analysed control orders from a legal perspective, the second part of this research aims to explore both the rationale giving rise to the problematic legal hybrids, as well as the opportunity-reducing mechanisms underlying the control order restrictions themselves. Before turning our attention to comparing control order mechanisms to those of situational crime prevention, the following chapter examines how risk has evolved from actuarial predictions based on past conduct towards a more precautionary approach to deal with the inherent uncertainty of trying to prevent terrorist attacks.

---

[43] For Thomas, see Hayne J at 485.

References

Anderson, D. (2012). Control orders in 2011: Final Report of the Independent Reviewer on the Prevention of Terrorism Act 2005. London: The Stationary Office.

Australian Associated Press. (2007). PM defends Hicks' retrospective charge, *The Age*. Retrieved from http://www.theage.com.au/news/National/PM-defends-Hicks-retrospective-charge/2007/02/04/1170523946635.html.

Bennett, D. (2007). *Thomas v Mowbray: The constitutionality of control orders*. Paper presented at the 35th Australian Legal Convention, Sydney. http://www.lawcouncil.asn.au/shadomx/apps/fms/fmsdownload.cfm?file_uuid=E40874B3-1E4F-17FA-D2B1-E7C05BE5421B&siteName=lca.

Bonner, D. (2006). Checking the executive? Detention without trial, control orders, due process and human rights. *European Public Law*, *12*(1), 45–71.

Carlile of Berriew, A. (2006). First Report of the Independent Reviewer pursuant to Section 14(3) of the Prevention of Terrorism Act 2005. London: HMSO.

Constitutional Affairs Committee. (2005). The operation of the special immigration appeals commission (SIAC) and the use of special advocates. Seventh Report of Session 2004–2005. London: The House of Commons.

Hicks, D. (2010). *Guantanamo: my journey*. Sydney: Random House Publishing.

International Commission of Jurists. (2009). Assessing damage, urging action: Report of the Eminent Jurists Panel on Terrorism, Counter-terrorism and Human Rights. In I. C. o. Jurists (Ed.). Geneva: International Commission of Jurists.

Ip, J. (2007). Comparative perspectives on the detention of terrorist suspects. *Transnational Law and Contemporary Problems*, *16*, 773–871.

Jaggers, B. (2008). Anti-terrorism control orders in Australia and the United Kingdom: A comparison. Canberra: Parliamentary Library, Department of Parliamentary Services.

Kavanagh, A. (2010). Special advocates, control orders and the right to a fair trial. *The Modern Law Review*, *73*(5), 824–857.

Lasry, L. (2007). *United States v David Matthew Hicks*: Final Report of the Independent Legal Observer for the Law Council of Australia Canberra, Law Council of Australia.

Lynch, A. (2006b). Maximising the drama: 'Jihad Jack', the court of appeal and the Australian media. *Adelaide Law Review*, *27*, 311–334.

Lynch, A. (2008). Thomas v Mowbray. [Case note]. *Melbourne University Law Review*, *32*, 1182–1211.

Macdonald, S. (2007). ASBOs and control orders: Two recurring themes, two apparent contradictions. *Parliamentary Affairs*, *60*(4), 601–624.

Walker, C. (2011). *Terrorism and the law*. Oxford: Oxford University Press.

Zedner, L. (2007b). Preventive justice or pre-punishment? The case of control orders. *Current Legal Problems*, *60*(1), 174–203. doi: 10.1093/clp/60.1.174.

Chapter 5
The Changing Face of Risk

5.1 Introduction

The previous chapters have highlighted that much of the criticism arising from control orders stems from their lack of adherence to procedural safeguards. Yet, both the British and Australian governments have described control orders as a necessary tool to protect their citizens from the enormous and uncertain risk posed by terrorism. Indeed, risk is the underlying rationale and justification for the state's protective mandate (Aradau and van Munster 2007; Feeley and Simon 1992), and its use of exceptional measures. Modern states have a duty to protect their citizens (Ashworth 2009), but there has been a long debate about how they go about doing so.[1] In recent years, risk has evolved, moving toward assessment and management of risky populations, introducing a more preventive focus in criminal justice. The rise of actuarial approaches in criminal justice has also filtered into the debate on terrorism, preventive legislation being just one example thereof. This chapter expands on risk as it applies to terrorism and the development and implementation of (pre-emptive) Anti-Terrorism legislation.

5.2 Pre 9/11

Writing in the early 1990s, Feeley and Simon (1992) observed a shift in penal discourse toward risk and probability. The 'new penology', as they called it, saw a desistence from the traditional focus on the individual (his/her moral or clinical portrayal) to a more aggregate level, focusing resources into the identification, classification and management of groups, ultimately for the purposes of surveillance, confinement and control (Feeley and Simon 1992). Punishment and rehabilitation were replaced with managing dangerous groups via prediction tools and statistical indicators, resulting in custodial institutions becoming vessels of risk

[1] See for example, Hobbes (1651), Locke (1690) and Hindess (1996).

S. Donkin, *Preventing Terrorism and Controlling Risk*, Springer Briefs in International and Comparative Criminology, DOI: 10.1007/978-1-4614-8705-0_5,

containment for potentially dangerous categories of individuals, for example sex offenders, until their level of risk is assessed and controlled (Rose 2000). Shearing (2001) elucidated how the justification of prison, originally perceived as a deterrent, thus shifted toward incapacitation, signalling the end of the punishment paradigm. Instead, it evolved into a tool for the minimisation of harm to others, and thus, risk management (Shearing 2001).

A growing body of literature is concerned with risk, its assessment and management (Zedner 2006). Risk indicates the likelihood of damage, harm or danger (Mythen and Walklate 2006). The probability of risk is calculated by using past events to predict future outcomes, predominantly using statistical techniques. However, given the inherent uncertainty of whether or not these predictions actually come to pass, Mythen and Walklate ascribe the power of risk in the potential of a risk occurring. The actuarial character of this trend was heavily influenced by economics and business models, explaining the new focus on regulation rather than intervention or response (Feeley and Simon 1992). Beck previously described this escalating prevalence of risk as resulting in a 'risk society', where risk is defined as "a systematic way of dealing with hazards and in securities" (1992, p. 21). Indeed, the concept of risk is clearly evident in our reaction to crime (Kennedy and Gibbs Van Brunschot 2009). The incorporation of the term risk has, according to some observers, led to discourses becoming more technically sophisticated (Loader and Sparks 2002). Yet, as Beck (2002) highlighted, attempting to calculate certain types of risk or the occurrence of a particular event can be akin to calculating the incalculable, making the presumption of risk inherently political (Loader and Sparks 2002; Zedner 2006), and thus driven by the political climate of the time. Certainly, innovative techniques and novel language have contributed to reconceptualised policies (Feeley and Simon 1992).

The emergence of the risk-oriented approach brought with it an increased focus on trying to prevent events (Shearing 2001; Zedner 2009), resulting in the preventive detention of offenders, suspects, and even illegal immigrants. Rose (2000) suggested this trend developed in reaction to risky individuals who cannot be managed using conventional methods. Originally devised to manage and control the "underclass" or high risk group for the protection of society (Feeley and Simon 1992, p. 467; Rose 2000), risk management with its preventive responses began to replace rehabilitation and reintegration (Feeley and Simon 1994). In order to identify and classify risk, new and more economical forms of custodial control were developed, with investment into new technologies to monitor suspected populations (Feeley and Simon 1992). For instance, innovations in management included electronic surveillance and house arrest. In essence, both Beck (1992, 2002) and Braithwaite (2000) argued that we have developed into a risk society with an increasing emphasis on preventive governance.

Actuarial justice and traditional risk assessment is calculated on the basis of tangible and measurable facts. Feeley and Simon (1992) believe the new penology is the upshot of incremental enhancements in qualitative rigor. For example, the identification of habitual criminals as a separate class of dangerous offenders followed increased and more rigorous recording practices in the nineteenth century (Morris 1951; Pratt 1997).[2] However, these types of preventive measures were used to manage the risk posed by potentially dangerous offenders *after* release from prison, making this form of risk assessment reactive in nature. Importantly, the character of risk changes according to when in relation to crime commission it is considered (Kennedy and Gibbs Van Brunschot 2009).

Recently, some authors argued that risk-based approaches in public policy are being augmented or replaced by precautionary principles, i.e. protecting society against potential harms, even if they are uncertain in nature (Goldsmith 2008; Sunstein 2005; Zedner 2009). The greater reliance on actuarial techniques, however, has promoted precautionary logic as a precursor to dealing with known risk, thus affecting the legal mechanisms dealing with unfamiliar risks. Reminiscent of Donald Rumsfeld's infamous speech (Rumsfeld 2002),[3] this approach of preparing for "unknown unknowns" also lays the foundation for pre-emptive measures to be applied in cases where the threat or risk has not been established. Writing in 2001, Shearing hypothesised that the emerging emphasis on risk would bring about changes in the legal framework to allow the state to apply its risk strategies to what Kennedy and Gibbs Van Brunschot (2009) referred to as the anticipatory phase of risk. Although the notion of trying to pre-empt crime is not novel, Dershowitz (2006) argued the events of 9/11 have accelerated recent legal incarnations of pre-emption.

5.3 Post 9/11

The emergence of terrorism as a potent 'new' or perceived threat since 2001 has yet further extended the new trends in governance and actuarialism in criminal justice described above. The focus shifted from managing risk to controlling it (Hudson 2003; Mythen and Walklate 2006). Hudson (2003) described the difference as risk management recognising that risk cannot be eliminated, but attempting to manage it by making improvements, all the while accepting that errors are inevitable. Controlling risk, on the other hand, aims to take control of a risky situation to prevent a crime from happening. This extension of institutional control still relies on classification on the basis of aggregate characteristics, rather than on reliable predictions about the individual risk of offending, resulting in the

---

[2] More recently, incidents and locations of past crimes have been used to predict probable locations of future crimes (Johnson et al. 2009).

[3] "Reports that say that something hasn't happened are always interesting to me, because as we know, there are known knowns; there are things we know we know. We also know there are known unknowns; that is to say we know there are some things we do not know. But there are also unknown unknowns—the ones we don't know we don't know. And if one looks throughout the history of our country and other free countries, it is the latter category that tend to be the difficult ones."

construction of a suspect population (Mythen and Walklate 2006). In other words, aggregate calculations of risk are not based on expert opinions, rather an actuarial judgment whether or not the individual in question "possesses the characteristics associated with reoffending" (Hudson 2003, p. 48).

In addition to the probability of an event occurring, the magnitude and value of its outcome also affects the calculation of risk (Douglas 1992). Terrorism being a high consequence—low probability risk (Mythen and Walklate 2006) lead Aradau and van Munster (2007) to argue that traditional risk management needs to be permanently adjusted in light of the uncertainty of potential catastrophic events. Not knowing who, when or where will be attacked promotes what Kennedy and Gibbs Van Brunshot called "a general form of prevention against all possibilities" (2009, p. 59). In essence, the new paradigm is one based on pre-emption and uncertainty which applies coercive restrictions "on the basis of what is anticipated might happen in the future" (McCulloch 2006, p. 359). Some scholars interpreted terrorism and post 9/11 developments as supporting Beck's notion of the risk society (Beck 2002; Borgers and van Sliedregt 2009); being one step ahead of the perceived threat and taking preventive action even in the absence of certainty or imminence is seen as being merely an extension of Beck's thesis. However, Amoore and De Goede (2008) highlighted that while pre-emption might draw on actuarial language and techniques, it actually surpasses them. This view is also shared by Aradau and van Munster who stated that Beck's risk society does not acknowledge that identifying risk is "not the same as recognising the uncertainty of future events" (Aradau and van Munster 2007, p. 95).

The pre-emptive paradigm thrives in a climate of uncertainty and fear (Lendermann 2009; Sunstein 2005). Uncertainty is also at the heart of precaution, which is not dissimilar to pre-emption in that it licences action if unpredictable and grave harm is threatened (Zedner 2009). According to Stern and Wiener (2006), it is precisely the fact that precaution relates to unknown risks which distinguishes it from prevention. A popular concept in environmental studies since the 1970s, the precautionary principle, based on the German *Vorsorgeprinzip*, stipulates that in situations that threaten serious or irreversible damage, uncertainty or lack of evidence is no reason not to act (Borgers and van Sliedregt 2009; Stern and Wiener 2006; Sunstein 2003, 2005). Precautionary risk thus incorporates uncertainty and catastrophic consequences into the calculations of the future.

Aradau and van Munster stipulated that precautionary risk is the opposite of prudence, which advocates taking certain precautions in light of known facts or risks, as opposed to acting "under scientific and causal uncertainty" and imagining the worst case scenario (Aradau and van Munster 2009, p. 696). They referred to the inability to calculate this uncertain risk as governing "at the limit of knowledge" (Aradau and van Munster 2007, p. 91; Zedner 2009, p. 47). Yet, several scholars believe that fear of future harm is increasingly driving government strategies (Aradau and van Munster 2007; McSherry 2006; Sunstein 2005; Zedner 2006), leading Zedner (2009) to conclude that uncertainty has superseded risk as the leading predicament for governments. This view was also shared by Ericson (2007), observing that risk management and uncertainty caused a radical transformation of the traditional legal framework. Aradau and van Munster (2009) believe that this paradigm is also being transferred to law, which is usually enacted to something tangible and concrete, but is now being used to deal with a non-predictable future.

5.4 The Precautionary Rationale

Many of the issues identified in relation to control orders in the previous chapters appear to be indicative of this increased focus on managing uncertainty and applying precautionary responses. Ashworth and Zedner (2007) referred to this shift as contributing to the rise of the preventive state, which becomes an umbrella for all forms of prevention and pre-emption (Ashworth 2009). Terrorism in particular appears to have served as the justification for the expansion of the precautionary principle into the political arena (Mythen and Walklate 2006; Zedner 2006). Aradau and van Munster cogently argued that the precautionary principle favours rapid political decisions, which they contended was also a reason for governments choosing to act through a system of administrative decisions rather than the slower legal process. In their opinion, the shift toward precaution in reaction to terrorism is a new form of governmentality which embraces uncertainty, war and surveillance technologies, but does not rely solely on pre-emptive risk management in its bid to prevent future catastrophic events (Aradau and van Munster 2007). Several strategies are affected by this new rationality. Hudson (2003) argued that risk and its control has overtaken concerns about due process and proportionality. To highlight the effects of the precautionary principle on criminal law Ericson (2007) used the term counter-law.[4] He distinguished between two types of counter-law, the first describes introducing or amending existing laws to circumvent existing principles as part of the state of exception or to deal with increased uncertainty, whereas the second creates and extends surveillance networks to facilitate pre-emption (Ericson 2007). He also found that previously distinct categories of law, such as criminal, civil and administrative, have become blurred, evaporating legal safeguards in the process (Ericson 2007). Similarly Borgers and van Sliedregt (2009) identified four preventive characteristics of Anti-Terrorism legislation, which they believe

[4] Ericson adapted the term counter-law from earlier uses, by Foucault (1977), amongst others. However, as Levi (2009) highlighted, whereas Foucault used the term to compare law and the disciplines, Ericson focused on the pursuit of security.

developed as a result of the risk society's reliance on the precautionary principle, all of which are evident in Australia's legal response to terrorism[5]:

1. *Criminalising the preliminary stage of the offence*;
2. *Expanding investigative powers*;
3. *Expanding pre-trial detention*; *and*
4. *Using non-criminal measures to achieve a repressive effect.*

The final point, using non-criminal measures in a repressive way, can be illustrated with control orders. Control orders are in essence a strategy of precaution used to both manage and control individuals suspected of terrorist involvement, and as such, a technology to protect its citizens from terrorism. The control order's underlying rationale is to manage that risk by acting pre-emptively, before any harm can come to the state and its citizens, leading Aradau and van Munster (2007) to call it an example of "precautionary governance through risk" (p. 91). The precautionary rationale triggers the whole process, as the decision to impose control orders originates with the Executive on the basis of suspicion arising from intelligence materials. Relating back to Rumsfeld's infamous speech, Zedner (2009) described the orders as falling under the category of known unknowns, where pre-emptive measures are justified on the basis of uncertainty (Ericson 2007; Zedner 2009). Because the apparent terrorist attack has not yet materialised, traditional legal technologies, such as prosecution, are unavailable. In a traditional court of law, any reasonable doubt the judge and jury might have with regards to a defendant's guilt should result in a finding of not guilty (Ericson 2007). The precautionary logic, however, uses this uncertainty as the basis upon which to impose restrictions and sanctions. Zedner (2009) described control orders as institutionalising "uncertainty by enabling the state to impose restrictions upon suspects without exposing intelligence to the public scrutiny attendant upon prosecution" (p. 49). However, Ericson argued that allocating discretion to the administrative branch of government through administrative law is not unreasonable, as it is, in theory at least, well equipped to deal with uncertainty. Whereas previously such derogations from the norm were the exception, some critics argue that a constant state of uncertainty in an era of security appears to have justified counter-law measures taking on a more permanent form (Agamben 2005; Ericson 2007; Gross 2003, 2006; Michaelsen 2008).

---

[5] Australian anti-terrorism legislation not only criminalises acts done in preparation, but acts carried out even prior to an individual forming a criminal intent during what might be interpreted as preparation, thus expanding the traditional scope of criminal responsibility to a new level. Preparatory terrorism offences [s.101.5 *Criminal Code* (*Cth*)] are targeted at criminalising acts which precede even inchoate offences thereof (Gani 2008; Lynch 2006; McGarrity and Williams 2010). Traditionally, an attempt required a person's conduct to be "more than merely preparatory to the commission of the offence" (McSherry 2004, p. 366). Yet technically, McSherry (2004) highlighted the possibility that an individual might be charged with attempting to do an act in preparation for a terrorist act.

5.5 The Terrorism Emergency

Risk and uncertainty also shape the framework around exceptional circumstances requiring recourse to emergency powers. One of the frequently cited critiques of Anti-Terrorism legislation, particularly in the advent of 9/11, is that terrorism justifies exceptional laws under the guise of emergency. Emergency powers are invoked in times of crisis or emergency, when the ordinary legal framework is considered inadequate to accommodate for a change in circumstances. Declared by the Executive, these powers often include temporary derogations of fundamental rights and a shift in the established balance of power between the pillars of government (Aradau and van Munster 2009; Bonner 2006; Johns 2005; Lazar 2006). However, the terrorist threat differs from the traditional threats which were at the forefront at the time emergency legislation was conceived and applied. Most emergency legislation in Britain for instance was conceived to deal with internal disorder (such as strike situations), as well as instances affecting or threatening essential services.[6]

Several scholars have argued that distinguishing between normalcy and exception has become more challenging in the wake of 9/11 as the exception and its government becomes norm (Ackerman 2003; Agamben 2005; Bronitt and McSherry 2010; Ericson 2007; Gross 2003; Gross and Ní Aoláin 2006; Lynch et al. 2010; Moran 2007; Welch 2007). The term emergency usually signifies a temporary event (Boyle 1982; Gross and Ní Aoláin 2006). However, emergencies have often been subject to renewal and extension, especially those related to terrorism.[7] Associated with terrorism's inherent uncertainty is the inability to foresee an end to the threat. Although the war metaphor is frequently used in relation to terrorism, wars in the 'conventional' sense have a clear end. In this sense, terrorism fits neither into the traditional perception of an emergency, nor into that of war. That being said, internment,[8] a war time measure originally enacted to deal with the management of suspect (alien) populations, was repeatedly used to detain suspected terrorists in Northern Ireland. Although an emergency can legally justify certain derogations to law and human rights, Michaelsen (2005) argued liberal democratic countries including Australia and the UK, having played pivotal roles in establishing common human rights standards, have a responsibility to uphold these, no matter how grave a crisis might appear.

---

[6] The key legislation was the *Emergency Powers Act 1920*, later amended by the *EPA 1964*.

[7] Several British anti-terrorism laws originated within an emergency framework, many of which were related to the situation in Ireland. Intended to be temporary, numerous statutes were eventually permanently adopted into the statute books (Donohue 2000; Walker 2011).

[8] Internment, i.e. detention with neither charge nor trial, dates back centuries (Bonner 2006; Lowry 1976). Internment in Northern Ireland was first introduced in 1922 under emergency legislation, the *Civil Authorities (Special Powers) Act (Northern Ireland) 1922*. It was last used in 1975, its legal basis, however, remained in the books until 1998.

5.6 The Evolution of Risk

Many observers argued that the security paradigm is increasingly being adopted and normalised to a degree never before seen (Agamben 2005; McCulloch 2009; McCulloch and Pickering 2009), changing the role of criminal law along the way (Ericson 2007). This transition is also evident in other areas of governance, expanding the boundaries of risk and uncertainty, creating hybrids of previously distinct areas of law, affecting the separation of powers, ultimately altering how emergencies and exceptions are conceived and implemented. Agamben stated that administrative governance appears to be increasing at the expense of the rule of law; with management triumphing in the absence of order (Raulff 2004). Anti-Terrorism legislation post 9/11, according to Zedner (2007), has been heavily influenced by the actuarial model of risk and uncertainty, a reflection of the age of security, leading some to comment that traditional measures of risk have been abandoned in favour of less democratic approaches to the governance of risk (Hudson 2009). Indeed, Ericson (2007) believed that law defines risk beyond the scientific threshold, thus entering the realm of uncertainty. That being said, the precautionary logic argues that uncertainty is no excuse for inaction and absence of evidence is not the same as absence of risk (De Goede and Randalls 2009). Having examined how the perceived increase in risk in the absence of evidence has shaped the creation of legal hybrids to control individuals suspected of posing a terrorist threat, the following chapter examines more traditional and, more importantly, less coercive techniques to reduce opportunities for crime.

References

Ackerman, B. (2003). The emergency constitution. *Yale Law Journal, 113*, 1029–1091.

Agamben, G. (2005). *State of exception*. Chicago: The University of Chicago Press.

Amoore, L., & De Goede, M. (2008). Introduction: Governing by risk in the war on terror. In L. Amoore & M. De Goede (Eds.), *Risk and the war on terror*. London: Routledge.

Aradau, C., & van Munster, R. (2007). Governing terrorism through risk: Taking precautions, (un)knowing the future. *European Journal of International Relations, 13*(1), 89–115. doi:10.1177/1354066107074290.

Aradau, C., & van Munster, R. (2009). Exceptionalism and the 'War on Terror'. *British Journal of Criminology, 49*, 686–701.

Ashworth, A. (2009). Criminal law, human rights and preventative justice. In B. McSherry, A. Norrie, & S. Bronitt (Eds.), *Regulating deviance: The redirection of criminalisation and the futures of criminal law*. Oxford and Portland OR: Hart Publishing.

Ashworth, A., & Zedner, L. (2007). Defending the criminal law: Reflections on the changing character of crime, procedure, and sanctions. *Criminal Law and Philosophy, 2*(1), 21–51.

Beck, U. (1992). *Risk society: Toward a new modernity*. London: Sage.

Beck, U. (2002). The terrorist threat: World risk society revisited. *Theory Culture Society, 19*(4), 39–55. doi:10.1177/0263276402019004003.

Bonner, D. (2006). Checking the executive? Detention without trial, control orders, due process and human rights. *European Public Law, 12*(1), 45–71.

Borgers, M., & van Sliedregt, E. (2009). The meaning of the precautionary principle for the assessment of criminal measures in the fight against terrorism. *Erasmus Law Review, 2*(2), 171–195.

Boyle, K. (1982). Human rights and political resolution in northern ireland. *Yale Journal of World and Public Order, 9*, 156–177.

Braithwaite, J. (2000). The new regulatory state and the transformation of criminology. *British Journal of Criminology, 40*(2), 222–238.

Bronitt, S., & McSherry, B. (2010). *Principles of criminal law* (3rd ed.). Sydney: Thomson Reuters.

De Goede, M., & Randalls, S. (2009). Precaution, preemption: Arts and technologies of the actionable future. *Environment and Planning D: Society and Space, 27*(5), 859–878.

Dershowitz, A. M. (2006). *Preemption: A knife that cuts both ways*. New York: W.W. Norton & Company.

Donohue, L. K. (2000). Civil liberties, terrorism, and liberal democracy: Lessons from the United Kingdom. BCSIA discussion paper 2000–2005. John F. Kennedy School of Government, Harvard University.

Douglas, M. (1992). *Risk and cultural theory*. London: Routledge.

Ericson, R. V. (2007). *Crime in an insecure world*. Cambridge: Polity Press.

Feeley, M. M., & Simon, J. (1992). The new penology: Notes on the emerging strategy of corrections and its implications. *Criminology, 30*(4), 449–474.

Feeley, M. M., & Simon, J. (1994). Actuarial justice: The emerging new criminal law. In D. Nelken (Ed.), *The future of criminology* (pp. 173–200). London: Sage.

Foucault, M. (1977). *Discipline and punish: The birth of the prison*. New York: Pantheon.

Gani, M. (2008). How does it end? Reflections on Completed prosecutions under Australia's Anti-Terrorism legislation. In M. Gani & P. Mathew (Eds.), *Fresh perspectives on the war on terror*. Canberra: ANU E Press.

Goldsmith, A. (2008). The governance of terror: Precautionary logic and counterterrorist law reform after September 11. *Law and Policy, 30*(2), 141–167.

Gross, O. (2003). Chaos and rules: Should responses to violent crises always be constitutional? *The Yale Law Journal, 112*(5), 1011–1134.

Gross, O. (2006). What "Emergency" regime? *Constellations, 13*(1), 74–88. doi:10.1111/j.1351-0487.2006.00441.x.

Gross, O., & Ní Aoláin, F. (2006). *Law in times of crisis: Emergency powers in theory and practice*. Cambridge: Cambridge University Press.

Hindess, B. (1996). *Discourses of power*. Oxford: Blackwell Publishers Ltd.

Hobbes, T. (1651). Leviathan. London: Penguin Classics.

Hudson, B. (2003). *Justice in the risk society*. London: Sage Publications.

Hudson, B. (2009). Justice in a time of terror. *British Journal of Criminology, 49*, 702–717.

Johns, F. (2005). Guántanamo bay and the annihilation of the exception. *European Journal of International Law, 16*(4), 613–635. doi:10.1093/ejil/chi135.

Johnson, S., Bowers, K., Birks, D. J., & Pease, K. (2009). Predictive mapping: Accuracy for different units of analysis and the role of the environmental backcloth. In D. Weisburd, W. Bernasco, & G. J. N. Bruinsma (Eds.), *Putting crime in it's place: Units of analysis in spatial crime research*. Dordrecht: Springer.

Kennedy, L. W., & Gibbs Van Brunschot, E. (2009). *The risk in crime*. New York: Rowman and Littlefield.

Lazar, N. C. (2006). Must exceptionalism prove the rule? An angle on emergency government in the history of political thought. *Politics & Society, 34*(2), 245–275. doi:10.1177/0032329205285406.

Lendermann, M. (2009). Prävention durch Recht—Kann normative auf terrorismus reagiert werden? (Prevention through law: Can one react normatively to terrorism?). Humbolt Forum Recht (12), 163-175.

Levi, R. (2009). Making counter-law. *British Journal of Criminology, 49*(2), 131–149. doi:10.1093/bjc/azn080.

Loader, I., & Sparks, R. (2002). Contemporary landscapes of crime, order and control: Governance, risk and globalization. In M. Maguire, R. Morgan, & R. Reiner (Eds.), *The oxford handbook of criminology* (3rd ed.). Oxford and New York: Oxford University Press.

Locke, J. (1690). Two treatises of government. Cambridge: Cambridge University Press.

Lowry, D. R. (1976). Internment: Detention without trial in Northern Ireland. *Human Rights, 5*, 261–331.

Lynch, A. (2006). Legislating with urgency—the enactment of the Anti-Terrorism Act [No 1] 2005. *Melbourne University Law Review, 30*(3), 747–781.

Lynch, A., McGarrity, N., & Williams, G. (2010). The emergence of a 'culture of control'. In N. McGarrity, A. Lynch, & G. Williams (Eds.), *Counter-terrorism and beyond: The culture of law and Justice after 9/11*. London: Routledge.

McCulloch, J. (2006). Australia's Anti-Terrorism legislation and the jack thomas case. *Current Issues in Criminal Justice, 18*(2), 357–365.

McCulloch, J. (2009). Precrime: Imagining future crime and a new space for criminology. Paper presented at the Australia and New Zealand Critical Criminology Conference, Melbourne. http://arts.monash.edu.au/criminology/c3-conference-proceedings/anz-critical-criminology-conference-2009-proceedings.pdf.

McCulloch, J., & Pickering, S. (2009). Pre-crime and counter-terrorism: Imagining Future crime in the 'War on Terror'. *British Journal of Criminology, 49*, 628–645.

McGarrity, N., & Williams, G. (2010). When extraordinary measures become normal: Pre-emption in counter-terrorism and other laws. In N. McGarrity, A. Lynch, & G. Williams (Eds.), *Counter-terrorism and beyond: The culture of law and justice after 9/11*. London: Routledge.

McSherry, B. (2004). Terrorism offences in the criminal code: broadening the boundaries of australian criminal laws. *University of New South Wales Law Journal, 27*(2), 354–372.

McSherry, B. (2006). Sex, drugs and 'evil' souls: The growing reliance on preventive detention regimes. *Monash University Law Review, 32*(2), 237–274.

Michaelsen, C. (2005). International human rights on trial—the United Kingdom's and Australia's legal response to 9/11. *Sydney Law Review, 25*(3), 275–303.

Michaelsen, C. (2008). The proportionality principle in the context of Anti-Terrorism laws: An inquiry into the boundaries between human rights law and public policy. In M. Gani & P. Mathew (Eds.), *Fresh perspectives on the 'War on Terror'* (pp. 109–124). Canberra: ANU E Press.

Moran, J. (2007). Generating more heat than light? Debates on civil liberties in the UK. *Policing, 1*(1), 80–93. doi:10.1093/police/pam009.

Morris, N. (1951). *The habitual criminal*. London: Longmans, Green and Co.

Mythen, G., & Walklate, S. (2006). Criminology and terrorism. *British Journal of Criminology, 46*(3), 379–398. doi:10.1093/bjc/azi074.

Pratt, J. (1997). *Governing the dangerous: Dangerousness, law and social change*. Sydney: The Federation Press.

Raulff, U. (2004). An Interview with Giorgio Agamben. *German Law Journal, 5*(5), 609–614.

Rose, N. (2000). Government and control. *British Journal of Criminology, 40*(2), 321–339.

Rumsfeld, D. (2002). US Department of Defence news briefing—secretary Rumsfeld and gen. Myers.

Shearing, C. (2001). Punishment and the changing face of the governance. *Punishment and Society, 3*(2), 203–220.

Stern, J., & Wiener, J. B. (2006). Precaution against terrorism. *Journal of Risk Research, 9*(4), 393–447.

Sunstein, C. R. (2003). Beyond the precautionary principle. *University of Pennsylvania Law Review, 151*(3), 1003–1058.

Sunstein, C. R. (2005). *Laws of fear: Beyond the precautionary principle*. Cambridge: Cambridge University Press.

Walker, C. (2011). *Terrorism and the law*. Oxford: Oxford University Press.

Welch, M. (2007). Sovereign impunity in america's war on terror: Examining reconfigured power and the absence of accountability. *Crime, Law and Social Change, 47*(3), 135–150.
Zedner, L. (2006). Neither safe nor sound? The perils and possibilities of risk. *Canadian Journal of Criminology and Criminal Justice, 48*(3), 423–434.
Zedner, L. (2007). Pre-crime and post-criminology. *Theoretical Criminology, 11*, 261–281.
Zedner, L. (2009). Fixing the future? The pre-emptive turn in criminal justice. In B. McSherry, A. Norrie, & S. Bronitt (Eds.), *Regulating deviance: The redirection of criminalisation and the futures of criminal law*. Oxford and Portland OR: Hart Publishing.

Chapter 6
Crime Prevention: Back to Basics

6.1 Introduction

The previous chapters have highlighted how the risk of unpredictable and grave harm has been used to construct controversial legal hybrids aimed at preventing terrorist attacks. Exemplified by control order regimes in the UK and Australia, this precautionary approach to anti-terrorism law has been repeatedly challenged, resulting in the abolishment and replacement of the British scheme and reviews of Australian anti-terrorism laws. One of the principal criticisms levelled at control orders has been the extent of restrictions and obligations imposed on individuals who are suspected of posing a terrorist threat, but have not been found guilty of any offence. Traditionally, preventive restrictions of this magnitude have been reserved for individuals whose previous criminal conduct has indicated that they pose an exceptional risk to the general population. In the case of controlees, however, such risk assessments are inherently intelligence-based, a lack of evidence precluding criminal prosecution.

Control order restrictions are designed to prevent a controlee from engaging in terrorist-related activities. When subject to a control order, controlees are required to adhere to restrictions on movement and association, which aim to disrupt opportunities to engage in terrorist activity, and/or increase the risks of detection. In this way, the control order bears distinct similarities with several crime prevention strategies; in particular, situational crime prevention (SCP), a crime control strategy developed in the early 1980s (Clarke 1983). SCP aims to better understand the proximal "situational" causes of crime, suggesting that these are easier to both identify and manipulate than other more distal causes for criminal involvement. As such, SCP aims to reduce crime by reducing opportunities for crime.

The following chapter describes this situational approach to crime prevention, summarises several theoretical propositions that underlie it, outlines the key techniques it employs to prevent crime, and provides a number of illustrative examples of SCP interventions. The chapter concludes by considering the parallels that exist between SCP and the control orders discussed previously; in doing so, it

S. Donkin, *Preventing Terrorism and Controlling Risk*, Springer Briefs in International and Comparative Criminology, DOI: 10.1007/978-1-4614-8705-0_6,

provides an example of how the SCP approach can be applied to regulatory interventions, thus highlighting the potential for these differing approaches to inform one another.

6.2 Opportunity Theories

Situational crime prevention is informed by a number of theoretical approaches. These include the routine activity approach (Cohen and Felson 1979), the rational choice perspective (Cornish and Clarke 1986), and crime pattern theory (Brantingham and Brantingham 1993), often collectively referred to as the opportunity theories (Wortley and Mazerolle 2011). Unlike many traditional criminological approaches, the opportunity theories focus on the crime event itself and the immediate situation giving rise to it, i.e. opportunities for crime (Wortley and Mazerolle 2011). The routine activity approach depicts the crime event as a spatio-temporal convergence of three necessary components: a motivated offender, a suitable target and the absence of capable crime controllers (i.e. those who might prevent crime). Crime pattern theory focuses on when and where these convergences occur, incorporating the environment as the backcloth of opportunity. In the event of a convergence, the rational choice perspective outlines an offender decision calculus that draws upon proximal cues (pre-crime variables) to assess the suitability of available criminal opportunities. Specific localised situational factors, such as provocations, temptations and incentives, so-called situational precipitators (Wortley 2001), may also influence an offenders decision-making. Unified around the notion that a crime event results from the exploitation of criminal opportunity, the primary goal of the opportunity theories is to inform crime prevention strategies to prevent or remove opportunities for offending. Drawing on the routine activity approach, the crime event can be visually depicted as an interaction of three elements: victim/target, offender and location. This interaction is often referred to as the crime or problem triangle (see Fig. 6.1).

6.2.1 Crime Controllers

Originally, the guardian was the only actor capable of controlling crime identified in the routine activity approach. Guardians are someone or something capable of preventing the crime event—a security guard, police officer, or more frequently an ordinary citizen (Felson 2002). More recently, however, animate guardians are being replaced by electronic mechanisms, such as alarm systems, CCTV cameras, even electronic monitoring tags, many of which are also a more visible reminder of guardianship (Cusson 2002).

Updating the approach, Felson (1986) incorporated elements of Hirschi's (1969) control theory, identifying another crime controller—the handler. Handlers

Fig. 6.1 The crime or problem triangle (Sampson et al. 2010)

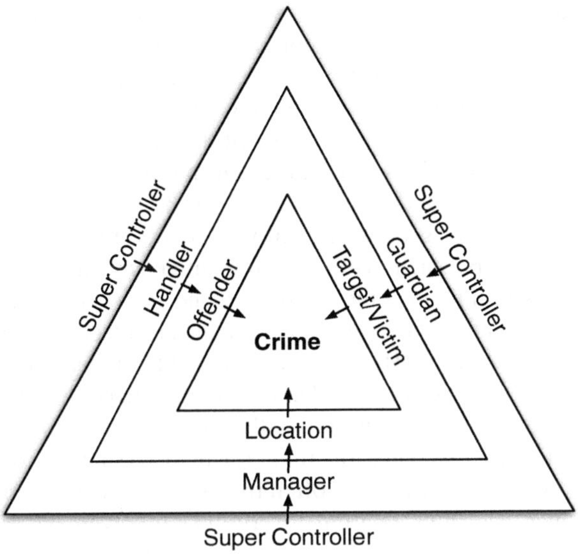

are individuals able to exert a degree of control and dissuasion over the offender due to a particular relationship or emotional attachment, such as a parent, spouse, friend or teacher, Subsequently, Eck (1993) proposed a further final controller—the place manager—capable of controlling crime at a particular location by controlling offender access to it, or challenging an offender's ability to offend within it. Examples of place managers include landlords, homeowners or tenants, shop attendants or bar staff. Unifying these three controllers with each respective element of the original crime triangle completes the second layer of the crime triangle—crime controllers. In response, Felson again updated his initial formulation of the crime convergence such that "crime occurs when the offender escapes handlers, finds targets free from guardians in settings not watched by managers" (Felson 2008, p. 74). Importantly, the identification and inclusion of the crime controller has become a significant part of crime prevention (Sampson et al. 2010).

Furthermore, Sampson, Eck and Dunham suggested that the controllers themselves could be given incentives to prevent crime by individuals or institutions (Sampson et al. 2010). Adding a third layer to the crime triangle, these 'super controllers' effectively control the controllers. Super controllers are not able to affect the conditions for a particular offence or offender, rather they exert their influence via guardians, managers and handlers. Just as an offender's decision to offend relies on the principles of rational choice, so too do a controller's on when to control. Super controllers aim to influence these decisions by manipulating incentives, e.g. increasing the rewards for implementing crime prevention, or alternatively, increasing the penalties for non-compliance. Sampson et al. identified three different types of super controllers, all capable of influencing each other: formal, diffuse and personal. Formal super controllers use formal authority, be it legal, financial or social, within a recognised institutional setting, and include courts and regulatory controllers. The formal process defines the interaction between the controller and the super controller, often involving a formal appeal process. Examples include the courts and other regulatory agencies. Diffuse super controllers include political institutions and the media, who can influence crime prevention efforts via legislation, publicity or market pressure. Finally, personal super controllers are connected to the controller via personal and informal ties, such as peer groups or family members. Each controller may have several super controllers, each with differing influence, dictating that there may be multiple ways to influence the controller, and to varying degrees.

Recently, the roles of guardian and place manager have been the subject of several studies (Hollis-Peel et al. 2011; Madensen and Eck 2008; Reynald 2010). The concept of the handler, on the other hand, is comparatively underdeveloped by opportunity theorists (see Tillyer (2008) for a notable exception). A likely explanation for this omission might relate to a reluctance of those who aim to inform SCP to venture down a road often frequented by developmental and life course scholars, since decisions relating to criminal involvement may well be more difficult to manipulate than those associated with a particular crime event. Here however, I will argue that given the similarities that exist between SCP interventions and control orders, the role of the handler may well be further developed to describe legislated offender handling mechanisms. First, however, a brief overview of the practical applications of these theoretical propositions is necessary.

6.3 Key Techniques of Situational Crime Prevention

Drawing on the opportunity theories, and in particular the rational choice perspective, SCP aims to reduce crime by increasing the perceived efforts and risks involved in committing crime, as well as reducing perceived rewards, excuses and provocations for doing so (Clarke 1995; Clarke and Eck 2003). Clarke (2008) outlined three assumptions of SCP: (1) crime is the result of the interaction between situation and motivation; (2) crime is the result of a choice; and (3) opportunity facilitates the incidence of crime. As such, SCP stipulates that the opportunity can be identified and subsequently manipulated to prevent the crime event (Clarke 1983).

SCP is problem-orientated and thus aims to focus on one particular category of crime, and/or place of intervention at a time due to the different situational determinants that exist between crime types and locations (Clarke 2011). Indeed, Clarke (1983) specified three characteristics of SCP measures: "(1) [they are] directed at highly specific forms of crime (2) that involve the management, design or manipulation of the immediate environment in as systematic and permanent a way as possible, (3) so as to reduce the opportunities for crime and increase its risks as perceived by a wide range of offenders" (p. 225). Subsequently, Clare and Morgan (2009, p. 216) identified three further factors of SCP: "(a) they do not

Table 6.1 The 25 techniques of SCP

Increase effort	Increase risk	Reduce rewards	Reduce provocations	Remove excuses
Target harden	Extend guardianship	Conceal targets	Reduce frustrations and stress	Set rules
Control access to facilities	Assist natural surveillance	Remove targets	Avoid disputes	Post instructions
Screen exits	Reduce anonymity	Identify property	Reduce temptation and arousal	Alert conscience
Deflect offenders	Use place managers	Disrupt markets	Neutralize peer pressure	Assist compliance
Control tools/ weapons	Strengthen formal surveillance	Deny benefits	Discourage imitation	Control drug and alcohol

discriminate, instead impacting on all citizens equally; (b) they do not necessarily restrict human rights and freedoms under the guise of increased security; and (c) they do not simply result in the offenders picking the next-best target as a result of opportunity reduction."

There may be multiple strategies at one's disposal to manipulate the opportunity to commit crime. A range of scholars have contributed to the now 25 techniques for situational crime prevention (Clarke and Eck 2003; Clarke and Homel 1997; Wortley 2001). These techniques can be subdivided into five key mechanisms (increase effort, increase risks, reduce rewards, reduce provocations and remove excuses) for each of which five potential opportunity-reducing strategies are provided, as shown in Table 6.1.

SCP is most effective when multiple measures aimed at intervening at different points of the offence are implemented. Importantly, considering the decision-making processes involved in crime commission can reveal useful information for crime prevention. Recognising this observation, scripts originally developed in cognitive science, were applied to the crime commission process by Derek Cornish in 1994. Crime scripts explicitly articulate the decision-making process involved in a particular crime, specifying the actors, circumstances and components required during all stages, i.e. before, during, and after crime (Cornish 1994). For instance, a simple car theft involves preparation, target selection, entering vehicle, starting vehicle, driving away, disposal of vehicle. As such, crime scripts identify potential points of intervention during which to increase the effort and risk, and reduce the rewards, ultimately attempting to prevent the offender from ever reaching the crime commission stage, i.e., pre-empting the offence.

Yet, not all strategies are applicable for each crime type or location. For instance, according to Wortley and Smallbone (2006), predatory offenders are most difficult to deter as they are more likely driven by motivation, and are thus not simply reacting to the opportunity or situation. The identification of offender types in SCP takes into account the interaction between the offender and the situation, thus enabling more targeted prevention strategies (Wortley 2012; Wortley and Smallbone 2006).

6.4 SCP Interventions

There have been many successful SCP interventions, targeting a multitude of crime problems and employing a wide variety of SCP techniques. Clarke's (1997) seminal collection of successful case studies documents 23 interventions, targeting everything from property crime, nuisance phone calls and night-time economy violence to prostitution. As such, SCP is not just a blanket intervention that is applied to the environment to deter property crimes. Wortley and Smallbone (2006) for instance, pioneered the approach in relation to sexual offending, in particular, that of child sex offending.

SCP interventions have also been used to deter terrorists for a number of years, be it through security checks and metal detectors at airports, or the removal of litter bins on UK high streets. Post 9/11, the awareness around weaknesses in security was further heightened, prompting governments and private organisations alike to introduce new security measures to protect potentially vulnerable infrastructure. One of the first papers to apply an opportunity-focused approach to terrorism was by Roach et al. (2005). Adapting Ekblom's (2001) Conjunction of Criminal Opportunity framework to terrorism, the Conjunction of Terrorist Opportunity seeks to examine the more direct causes of terrorist acts, including opportunity, assets, and motivation. Subsequently, Clarke and Newman proposed that terrorism could be reduced by removing the opportunities for terrorist attacks (Clarke and Newman 2006). Tailoring principles of SCP and the attractiveness of products to potential terrorist targets, Clarke and Newman (2006) identified four pillars of terrorist opportunity: targets, weapons, tools (cars, mobile phones, credit cards) and facilitating conditions (social or physical arrangements). Building on the CRAVED[1] (Clarke 1999) typology of attractive or 'hot' products commonly applied to property crime, Clarke and Newman developed a similar classification acronym to identify terrorist target attractiveness/vulnerability (EVIL DONE—Exposed, Vital, Iconic, Legitimate, Destructible, Occupied, Near, Easy) and attributes of weapons influencing a terrorist's decision (MURDEROUS—Multi-purpose, Undetectable, Removable, Destructive, Enjoyable, Reliable, Obtainable, Uncomplicated, Safe). SCP was thus adapted to become the situational prevention of terrorism (SPT).

Just as SCP is not overly concerned with why people burgle houses (acknowledging that sources of criminal motivation are diverse, but understandable), SPT is not concerned with the political motivations driving terrorists. That being said, Clare and Morgan argued that situational precipitators are indeed relevant to terrorism, precisely because of the underlying ideological motivation. Whilst a potential terrorist is likely highly motivated and prepared, he does not fit the description of a predatory offender either. According to Wortley and Smallbone (2006), the predatory offender will also commit opportunistic and situational offences; whereas terrorist offences, on the other hand, require a greater degree of planning (Clarke and Newman 2006).

[1] Concealable, Removable, Available, Valuable, Enjoyable and Disposable.

From suicide bombings (Clarke and Newman 2006) and biological attacks (Clark 2009) to murders of law enforcement personnel by right-wing extremists (Freilich and Chermak 2009), script analysis has also been applied to terrorism. Of particular relevance here is Hancock and Laycock's (2010) application of crime scripts to enhance understanding of organised crime so as to inform and facilitate prevention and disruption efforts. They highlighted that despite each discrete criminal act possessing its own unique, often offender-related features, sufficient shared elements exist, thus permitting generalisations capable of informing intervention strategies applicable to an entire class of offender. Hancock and Laycock broke down organised crime scripts into three parallel processes: criminal lifestyles, the primary criminal act(s), and groups and networks. The criminal lifestyle includes activities such as using false bank accounts and money laundering, in other words, activities which may exist independently of the primary criminal act. Groups and networks may be hierarchical in structure, or simply a network of associates. Hancock and Laycock argued that although most police investigations focus on the central pillar (gathering evidence about the criminal act in order to secure a conviction)[2] there is merit in focusing greater attention on the other pillars. Examining the interaction between the three pillars and focusing on pre-existing criminal lifestyle and criminal networks potentially supporting organised crime conditions "may present three separate but interrelated streams of opportunity for preventative/disruptive effort" (p. 177). The same principle can be applied to terrorism, and certainly, is apparent in control order strategies.

Before examining how SCP/SPT relates to control orders, it is important to highlight the role of legislation in crime prevention. The selection of examples above emphasises SCP's broad and diverse applications. However, whilst SCP interventions are varied, most are the result of measures introduced by government agencies, corporations or private citizens. It is much less common for SCP interventions to be formalised in regulation, even less so in legislation, despite Clarke and Newman's (2006) assertion that changes in legislation and judicial amendments are strategies able to work in conjunction with opportunity reducing techniques. Research in this area is even scarcer. In a notable exception,[3] Nelen (2010) scrutinised three projects aimed at preventing organised crime in Amsterdam, all of which used an administrative approach. Containing both preventive and repressive dimensions, the threefold strategy aiming to reduce opportunities for money laundering and crime was further supported with legislation that allowed for decisions on public tenders and contracts to be refused or withdrawn if there is a risk that these could lead to criminal acts or financial benefits

[2] They acknowledge that the response to organised crime has been broadened beyond enforcement with the introduction of serious crime prevention orders (SCPOs) in the UK, and increasing deportations of foreign nationals on the basis of intelligence alone.

[3] More recently, Eck and Eck (2012) applied a regulatory approach to place-based crime prevention. Drawing on environmental regulatory policy, Eck and Eck proposed tackling crime at places as a form of pollution, and devising regulatory policies similar to pollution control to crime places.

obtained from criminal activities (Nelen 2010). Nelen examined which of the 25 SCP techniques featured in Amsterdam's administrative approach. He found that the most popular strategies focused on increasing the effort and risks, and reducing rewards, to the detriment of removing excuses and, in particular, reducing provocations. Much like Nelen applied SCP techniques to administrative interventions, SCP can also be applied to the examination of control orders. The degree to which the 25 techniques are applicable is examined in the subsequent chapter.

6.5 Opportunities for Prevention

The theoretical propositions of the opportunity theories highlight the importance of individuals' routine activities and the decision processes involved in the commission of crime. Implemented in the form of situational crime prevention, both the rational choice perspective and routine activities approach inform practical approaches to crime prevention. Identifying particular offender types in SCP may be a fairly recent development, but allows for more targeted prevention strategies (Wortley and Smallbone 2006). Moreover, using crime scripts to identify commonly used tools and resources highlights potential points of intervention. Whilst the heterogeneous pool of controlees may be limited in number, the restrictions and obligations contained in control orders indicate the British and Australian governments' belief that there are sufficient shared elements to inform prevention strategies applicable to all controlees. Control orders aim to disrupt the pre-crime phase, removing opportunities to offend by preventing individuals from engaging in particular activities necessary or likely to facilitate terrorist activity. As such, they target all three of Hancock and Laycock's pillars—criminal lifestyle, (preparation) of criminal acts, and groups and networks.

Most of the implementations discussed above are examples of what Brantingham and Faust (1976) called primary crime prevention, where prevention efforts focus on altering the physical environment providing the opportunities for crime. Importantly, primary crime prevention also extends to the social environment, and as such, legislation, regulation and policy can all be described as a primary intervention techniques (Clare and Morgan 2009). Consequently, the statutory bases for control orders, i.e. the *Prevention of Terrorism Act 2005* and the *Anti-Terrorism (No. 2) Act 2005*, constitute primary crime prevention interventions. Secondary crime prevention, on the other hand, identifies potential offenders early and intervenes to prevent them from offending. A control order is thus an example of secondary crime prevention, as the order is targeted at an individual suspect in an effort to prevent them from engaging in terrorist activity.[4] The following chapter examines how SCP

[4] Tertiary crime prevention deals with the actual offender and aims to prevent recidivism, and is thus not relevant to this research.

mechanisms are indeed inherent in 'offender'-focused control orders, and thus, how the pre-emptive legal approach fits into the framework of situational crime prevention.

References

Brantingham, P. J., & Brantingham, P. L. (1993). Environment, routine and situation: Toward a pattern theory of crime. *Advances in Criminological Theory, 5*, 259–294.

Brantingham, P. J., & Faust, F. L. (1976). A conceptual model of crime prevention. *Crime and Delinquency, 22*(3), 284–296.

Clare, J., & Morgan, F. (2009). Exploring parallels between situational prevention and non-criminological theories for reducing terrorist risk. In J. D. Freilich & G. R. Newman (Eds.), *Reducing terrorism through situational crime prevention* (Vol. 25, pp. 207–227). Monsey: Criminal Justice Press.

Clark, W. (2009). Bioterrorism: A situational crime prevention approach. In J. D. Freilich & G. R. Newman (Eds.), *Reducing terrorism through situational crime prevention* (pp. 93–109). Monsey: Criminal Justice Press.

Clarke, R. V. (1983). Situational crime prevention: Its theoretical basis and practical scope. *Crime and Justice, 4*, 225–256.

Clarke, R. V. (1995). Situational Crime Prevention. *Crime and justice: A review of research, 19, Building a Safer Society: Strategic Approaches to Crime Prevention*, pp. 91–150.

Clarke, R. V. (Ed.). (1997). *Situational crime prevention: Successful case studies* (2nd ed.). Monsey: Criminal Justice Press.

Clarke, R. V. (1999). Hot products: Understanding, anticipating and reducing demand for stolen goods. London: Home Office, Police Research Series, Paper 112.

Clarke, R. V. (2008). Situational crime prevention. In R. Wortley & L. Mazerolle (Eds.), *Environmental criminology and crime analysis*. London: Routledge.

Clarke, R. V. (2011). Situational crime prevention. In R. Wortley & L. Mazerolle (Eds.), *Environmental criminology and crime analysis* (2nd ed.). Abingdon: Routledge.

Clarke, R. V., & Eck, J. E. (2003). *Become a problem-solving analyst in 55 small steps*. London: Jill Dando Institute of Crime Science, University College London.

Clarke, R. V., & Homel, R. (1997). A revised classification of situational crime prevention techniques. In S. P. Lab (Ed.), *Crime prevention at a crossroads* (pp. 17–27). Cincinnati: Anderson Publishing Co.

Clarke, R. V., & Newman, G. R. (2006). *Outsmarting the terrorists*. Westport: Praeger Security International.

Cohen, L. E., & Felson, M. (1979). Social change and crime rate trends: A routine activity approach. *American Sociological Review*, 588–608.

Cornish, D. B. (1994). The procedural analysis of offending and its relevance for situational prevention. *Crime Prevention Studies, 3*, 151–196.

Cornish, D. B., & Clarke, R. V. (1986). *The reasoning criminal: Rational choice perspectives on offending*. New York: Springer.

Cusson, M. (2002). *Prévenir la délinquance : Les méthodes efficaces*. Paris: Presses Universitaires de France.

Eck, J. E. (1993). Police problems: The complexity of problem theory, research and evaluation. In J. Knutsson (Ed.), *Problem-oriented policing: From innovation to mainstream* (15th ed.). Monsey: Criminal Justice Press.

Eck, J. E., & Eck, E. (2012). Crime place and pollution: Expanding crime reduction options through a regulatory approach. *Criminology and Public Policy, 11*(2), 281–316.

Ekblom, P. (2001). The conjunction of criminal opportunity: A framework for crime reduction toolkits. *Policing and Reducing Crime Unit, Home Office, London, UK. Obtained from www. Crimereduction. gov. uk.*

Felson, M. (1986). Linking criminal choices, routine activities, informal control, and criminal outcomes. In *The reasoning criminal* (pp. 119–128). New York: Springer.

Felson, M. (2002). *Crime and everyday life* (3rd ed.). Thousand Oaks: Sage Publications.

Felson, M. (2008). Routine activity approach. In R. Wortley & L. Mazerolle (Eds.), *Environmental Criminology and Crime Analysis*. London: Routledge.

Freilich, J. D., & Chermak, S. M. (2009). Preventing deadly encounters between law enforcement and American far-rightists. In J. D. Freilich & G. R. Newman (Eds.), *Reducing terrorism through situational crime prevention*. Cullompton: Willan Publishing.

Hancock, G., & Laycock, G. (2010). Organised crime and crime scripts: Prospects for disruption. In K. Bullock, R. V. Clarke, & N. Tilley (Eds.), *Situational prevention of organised crimes*. Cullompton: Willan Publishing.

Hirschi, T. (1969). *Causes of delinquency*. Berkeley: University of California Press.

Hollis-Peel, M. E., Reynald, D. M., van Bavel, M., Elffers, H., & Welsh, B. C. (2011). Guardianship for crime prevention: A critical review of the literature. *Crime, Law and Social Change, 56*(1), 53–70.

Madensen, T. D., & Eck, J. E. (2008). Violence in bars: Exploring the impact of place manager decision-making. *Crime Prevention and Community Safety, 10*(2), 111–125.

Nelen, H. (2010). Situational organised crime prevention in Amsterdam: The administrative approach. In K. Bullock, R. V. Clarke, & N. Tilley (Eds.), *Situational prevention of organised crimes*. Cullompton: Willan Publishing.

Reynald, D. M. (2010). Guardians on guardianship: Factors affecting the willingness to supervise, the ability to detect potential offenders, and the willingness to intervene. *Journal of Research in Crime and Delinquency, 47*(3), 358–390.

Roach, J., Ekblom, P., & Flynn, R. (2005). The Conjunction of Terrorist Opportunity: A Framework for Diagnostic and Preventing Acts of Terrorism. *Security Journal, 18*(3), 7–25.

Sampson, R., Eck, J. E., & Dunham, J. (2010). Super controllers and crime prevention: A routine activity explanation of crime prevention success and failure. *Security Journal, 23*(1), 37–51.

Tillyer, M. S. (2008). *Getting a handle on street violence: Using environmental criminology to understand and prevent repeat offender problems.* University of Cincinnati. Security Council Resolution 1566, S/RES/1566 (2004), United Nations (2004).

Wortley, R. (2001). A classification of techniques for controlling situational precipitators of crime. *Security Journal, 14*(4), 63–82.

Wortley, R. (2012). Exploring the person-situation interaction in situational crime prevention. In N. Tilley & G. Farrell (Eds.), *The reasoning criminologist: Essays in honour of Ronald V. Clarke*. London: Routledge.

Wortley, R., & Mazerolle, L. (2011). Environmental criminology and crime analysis: situating the theory, analytic approach and application. In R. Wortley & L. Mazerolle (Eds.), *Environmental criminology and crime analysis*. Abingdon: Routledge.

Wortley, R., & Smallbone, S. (2006). Applying situational principles to sexual offenses against children. In R. Wortley & S. Smallbone (Eds.), *Situational prevention of child sexual abuse*. Cullompton: Willan Publishing.

Chapter 7
Executive Terrorism Prevention and Risk Control

7.1 Introduction

Control orders aim to prevent an individual from engaging in activities that could ultimately lead to them carrying out a terrorist attack. To do so, they impose restrictions or obligations on an individual suspected of terrorist involvement. As the previous legal analysis has highlighted, the degree to which these individuals are being restricted is extraordinary given that they have not been found guilty of any offence. Obligations ranging from regular reporting, travel and communication restrictions, and even curfews are hallmarks of control orders in both the UK and Australia. Having examined control orders from a legal perspective, the following chapter dissects the rationale and mechanisms that underlie them, and in doing so provides several appropriate analogues from both the opportunity theories and SCP. Drawing on the taxonomy of crime controllers and their associated 'super' equivalents, here I propose that the control order represents a hybrid 'executive handler' capable of directly influencing those who are deemed to pose significant risks to society.

7.2 Terrorism Prevention

Many obligations and restrictions contained within control orders can easily be interpreted in light of the opportunity theories and SCP. Given that many control order restrictions are focused around the controlee's movements, it is easy to see how these measures are designed to affect an individual's routine activities. Preventing the potentially motivated 'offender' from converging with a poorly guarded target eliminates the individual's opportunity to commit the crime. Several restrictions aim to prevent said convergence: curfews, forced relocation, travel restrictions and electronic tagging. In addition to controlling the controlee's ability to go about their normal lives, the enforcement of restrictions also provides a level of formal surveillance; suspects have been formally identified, and their movements

S. Donkin, *Preventing Terrorism and Controlling Risk*, Springer Briefs in International and Comparative Criminology, DOI: 10.1007/978-1-4614-8705-0_7,

are closely monitored to ensure compliance with conditions set out in the control order. The British requirement of forced relocation[1] altered how potential offenders went about finding suitable targets, removing them from familiar areas, known targets and potential associates. Of course, offenders would develop an awareness of their new activity spaces, identifying possible new targets sooner or later. However, access to potential accomplices would likely be minimised given increased distances and communication restrictions.

Much of the existing research in SCP has focused on place managers and, more recently, guardians. Comparatively few research efforts have focused on the role of the handler, who is able to exert influence over the potential offender. This is in part a result of SCP interventions frequently being aimed at protecting a target or a place. Conversely, control order restrictions are directed at specific individuals thought to pose a terrorist threat, meaning that preventative restrictions represent measures targeted at the offender side of the crime triangle. These restrictions are imposed by a court-approved executive order, which takes on a role similar to the handler. Felson (1995) might classify control orders as assigned handlers, since the order was created and assigned for the specific purpose of preventing the controlee from engaging in potential terrorist activities. However, Felson (1995) also characterised handlers as exerting informal social control. Given that a handler's role and influence is normally much less coercive or authoritative than a control order is, I propose that control orders should thus be interpreted as executive handlers. Executive handlers provide a hybrid between handler and super handler, in that they are able to impose restrictions with the same authority as super handlers, but do so directly upon the individual. In considering the mechanisms by which the executive handler might coerce the potential offender, the following section outlines control orders in terms of SCP mechanisms.

7.2.1 SCP Mechanisms in Control Orders

In the immediate run up to a terrorist attack, the potential offender will consider characteristics of terrorist opportunities, such as target attractiveness and vulnerability, availability of weapons and tools, and facilitating conditions (Clarke and Newman 2006). Whilst these factors will inevitably influence an individual's decision to offend, the control order is not specifically designed to affect all of these elements. For instance, target attractiveness and vulnerability are more likely manipulated by traditional SCP interventions designed to protect iconic or vulnerable infrastructure. However, control order restrictions, such as prohibiting an individual's access to dangerous goods like explosives or weapons will increase the necessary effort to offend. Nevertheless, given that these goods are by their very nature rather more difficult to come by than the tools to commit a break and

[1] Forced relocation no longer features as part of the replacement TPIMs.

enter, as well as being more tightly controlled or prohibited, short of extended surveillance to ensure compliance or regular searches at the controlee's residence, this restriction appears somewhat superfluous as part of a control order.

Other restrictions, however, appear more persuasive. For instance, curfews increase the risk of detection by strengthening formal surveillance. They also remove excuses by setting clear rules around when an individual is allowed to leave the home, which in turn assists compliance. Indeed, a large proportion of controlee requirements constitute increases in risks of detection and/or the removal of excuses for certain prohibited activities. A frequently included obligation during non-curfew hours is to report to the local police station. Reporting requirements further increase risk by reducing anonymity, strengthening formal surveillance, and removing excuses by alerting the controlee's conscience. The latter rationale can also be said to be at work for fingerprinting, which in addition to reducing anonymity, also assists compliance. Travel restrictions increase a controlee's risk of apprehension by extending guardianship, using border control agents as place managers, who in turn strengthen formal surveillance.

The final group of restrictions, which relate to communications, encompass two further categories—increasing effort and reducing provocations. Restricting communications, such as access to the internet or mobile phone devices, controls an increasingly necessary tool in the preparation of a terrorist act; thus increasing the effort one must go to commutate with collaborators. Furthermore, given that permitted communication devices are likely to be monitored, such restrictions also increase guardianship and strengthen formal surveillance. Reducing excuses, restricting communication with certain individuals may neutralise peer pressure, and with no access to extremist websites, temptation and arousal may be reduced, in turn, discouraging imitation. In addition to the universal removing excuses by setting rules and assisting compliance, restricting communications also controls an important facilitator. Whilst the more traditional factors of drugs or alcohol may be less likely to play a role in terrorist-related cases, access to communications represents an equally important facilitator, distinguishable from controlling access to tools mentioned above due to the potential for emotional impact and effect comparable to drugs or alcohol, thus making it worthy of inclusion in both categories. Communication restrictions might also be framed by Wortley's situational precipitators. Limiting communication means that contact with potential associates or radical preachers is likely prohibited, removing the controlee from negative peer pressure to offend. The same logic holds true for restricting access to extremist websites or news stories of atrocities by allied forces. Restrictions on communications thus represent the only category of controls making use of four of the five SCP mechanisms. However, this statement is likely more a reflection of the pervasive nature of communications technology seen in today's society.

Table 7.1 summarises which SCP mechanisms apply to which control order obligation/restriction, highlighting that control orders rely heavily on two types of strategies, namely increasing risk and removing excuses. Increasing effort is only relevant where access to communications or restricted goods are controlled. Similarly, through SCP, provocations are only likely reduced by restricting

Table 7.1 SCP mechanisms used in control orders

	Increase effort	Increase risk	Reduce rewards	Reduce provocations	Remove excuses
Curfew		✔			✔
Travel restrictions		✔			✔
Reporting requirements		✔			✔
Fingerprinting		✔			✔
Restricting dangerous goods	✔	✔			
Restricting communications	✔	✔		✔	✔

communications. That being said, all means of restriction have the potential to increase frustration and stress for controlees.

While there are many parallels between control orders and SCP, the approaches also differ in a number of fundamental ways. Drawing on both Clarke's (2008) three characteristics of SCP, and Clare and Morgan's (2009) factors of SCP, Table 7.2 depicts a number of key differences between SCP interventions and control order restrictions.

Clarke states that SCP is directed at highly specific forms of crime. Whilst terrorism is one particular type of crime, terrorist attacks themselves can obviously take on a vast array of types. The term terrorism acts as an umbrella under which sit many different types of offences, from destruction of property to murder.[2] Moreover, any potential attack may well be unknown to authorities at the point of the control order, as specific information relating to a planned offence could be prosecuted under preparatory terrorist acts, thus invalidating the necessity to issue a control order. That being said, authorities may know details about an alleged plot, but lack sufficient evidence to prosecute the individual in question. A further distinction from SCP is that a control order targets one particular offender, rather than aiming to reduce a particular offence type at a specific location. Indeed, rather than manipulating the environment in a permanent way, control orders manage the controlee and his or her immediate environment only for the duration of the control order. Restrictions

[2] What might appear to be a straightforward and basic concept has proven difficult to define, with no universally accepted definition as yet (Lord Carlile of Berriew QC 2007). The political construction of what amounts to terrorism remains controversial and subjective. Despite requiring states to legislate against terrorism, the UN did not agree upon a common definition of what constitutes terrorism until October 2004 (Security Council Resolution 1566, United Nations, 2004). Internationally, there is considerable variation in both the definition of terrorism, and the way in which a state defines the associated offences. Both the Australian definitions of terrorist offences and their international counterparts have been described as broad, flexible, unclear and rather vague (Gani 2008; Lynch 2006, 2007; Lynch and McGarrity 2008; Lynch and Williams 2006; Security Legislation Review Committee 2006; Walker 2007; Zedner 2009). As a result, anti-terrorism offences may lack clear legislative intent (Lynch 2006), complicating practical applications. The lack of comparable definitions across nations only adds to this ambiguity, potentially impeding coordination between nations.

Table 7.2 Comparison of SCP and control order characteristics

SCP	Control order
Directed at highly specific forms of crime	Directed at the entire range of terrorism offences Directed at one particular individual
Manages or manipulates immediate environment in systematic and permanent way	Involves management of controlee and his immediate environment in a systematic but time-limited way
Reduces opportunities for crime and increases its risks to wide range of offenders	Reduces opportunities for terrorist offences for specific individual
Non-discriminatory, impacts individuals equally	Impacts on controlee (and his/her family)
Do not restrict human rights and freedoms under the guise of increased security	Restricts movement and imposes obligations based on the need to protect the public from a terrorist threat
Do not result in target displacement as a result of opportunity reduction	Do not result in target displacement as a result of opportunity reduction
Most effective when aimed at different points of the offence stage	Designed for the specific purpose to disrupt the pre-crime stage of a terrorist act

reduce opportunities to commit a terrorist act only for the individual placed under the order (and by extension their network), unless one considers that dissemination may provide a deterrent effect for other unknown but would-be terrorists. Whilst SCP interventions, according to Clare and Morgan, are non-discriminatory in that they affect everyone equally, control orders apply to a select few individuals only, who, in theory at least, have their restrictions tailored to their particular risk factors. Depending on the familial circumstances, a controlee's family may also be affected. A further distinction is that, unlike SCP interventions, control orders restrict an individual's movement. Clare and Morgan's final assertion that SCP does not result in offenders choosing the next best target as a result of the lack of opportunity, is in fact the only element which is equally applicable to control orders. It is unlikely that controlees could switch targets given that restrictions apply to them and not a particular target, and would thus be equally effective if new targets were selected. Finally, whilst SCP interventions are most effective when aimed at intervening at different points of the offence stage, control orders are specifically designed to disrupt the pre-emptive phase of a terrorist act.

Having established that control orders differ from SCP interventions in many respects, it may not be appropriate to describe them as SCP interventions, but to dismiss the similarities entirely would be equally inappropriate. Many differences arise from the shift in focus from the target and place to the 'offender'. The introduction of an executive handler closely monitoring and restricting individuals who have not been charged or found guilty of any offence adds a further layer of complexity to the concept of crime controllers. As the example of the control order highlights, this degree of intervention, normally reserved for individuals after a conviction, is being justified on the basis of the allegedly exceptional, yet uncertain risk they pose.

7.3 Controlling Risk

Chapter 5 demonstrated how the actuarial logic of risk management began to change the criminal justice landscape well before the events of 9/11. The unexpected feeling of vulnerability has lead to highly emotional responses in reaction to terrorism, and thus, governance through fear (Goldsmith 2008; Sunstein 2005). We have seen that precaution ushered in on the basis of uncertainty thus has potentially troublesome implications for criminal law (Emerton 2007; Ericson 2007; Zedner 2009). Actuarial techniques are now widely seen as being credible, having reached the same level of proof as is required in court (Zedner 2009). Although the risk of crime or terrorism is difficult to calculate (Zedner 2006), the threat of terrorism has become pervasive and the risk of potentially catastrophic events borne home by losses of life and property in successive signal events in New York, Madrid, Bali, London and Mumbai. The need to be seen to provide security and to be doing something against threats has driven governments to search for new and often controversial technologies and strategies. Some of these policies were sanctioned through assertions of uncertainty and exceptional risk (Aradau and van Munster 2009).

The emphasis of risk management and control over the past thirty years has evolved from focusing on the preventive management of dangerous groups of offenders for the purpose of surveillance and control, to precautionary strategies targeted at particular individuals. Certainly, control orders have yet further pushed this frontier by relying on intelligence information as the foundation for precautionary intervention. Concerned with future risks, intelligence is notoriously unreliable, in part due to the sheer volume of data (Manningham-Buller 2005; Roach 2010). While control orders were introduced to deal with the dangerous group du jour, i.e. terrorists, strategies used to control and manage this group are very much focused on the individual suspect. So while the alleged group affiliation provides the justification for suspending or affecting individual human rights, the effect has been relatively limited in terms of the number of individuals subjected to control orders.

In essence, the precautionary principle has shifted the focus from risk based on past events to potential risk in the future; from groups to individuals, changing general interventions to interventions targeted at specific individuals who might potentially pose a risk. It is this move towards the precautionary principle that has had me propose the executive handler, applying SCP mechanisms to control the controlees without any charge or conviction; justified on the basis of the uncertain risk allegedly posed by these individuals.

In summary, Fig. 7.1 depicts the relationship between intervention and risk. Traditionally, a proportionate relationship exists between severity of offence and level of intervention. In the case of criminal damage, for instance, the level of control is minimal, targeted at the environment and the intervention is general and non-coercive in nature. As offences increase in severity, generally the level of control increases. Throughout this process, the criminal safeguards remain stable.

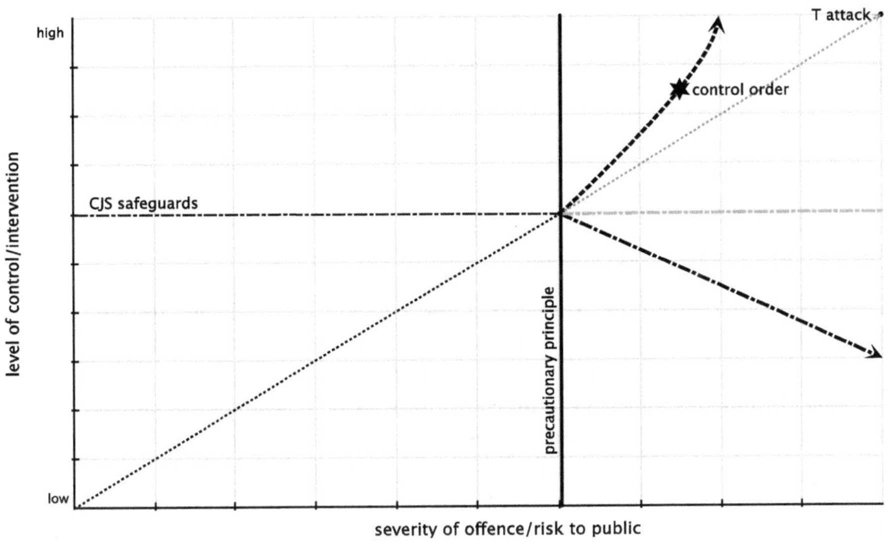

Fig. 7.1 The effect of the precautionary principle on the level of intervention

Terrorism, however, being a crime with potentially catastrophic consequences, invokes the precautionary principle at a much earlier stage than the actual terrorist event, i.e. in order to pre-empt it. At this point, the traditional relationship between severity of offence and the level of control diverts, increasing at an exponential rate and creating a jump in the level of control applied. At the same time, the previously stable criminal justice safeguards decrease. The control order sits along the exponentially increasing level of control invoked by the precautionary principle.

Examining the rationale and mechanisms underlying control orders has highlighted that, despite some fundamental differences, they share several key mechanisms with SCP. Most of the control order restrictions aim to prevent a convergence between a potentially motivated individual with an inadequately guarded target. The two key SCP mechanisms relied upon to do so are increasing risk and removing excuses. As part of the removal of excuses, several restrictions set clear rules, in turn, also assisting compliance. Clearly articulated obligations are particularly important so as not to breach any conditions of the control order, thus criminalising the breach and risking imprisonment. However, as Zedner (2007) highlighted, this was not always the case. Unlike SCP, however, the focus is no longer on the environment but on the controlee and his/her immediate home and social environment.

Enabled via a hybrid crime controller in the form of the executive handler, the extraordinary magnitude of a potential terrorist attack has been used to justify extraordinarily restrictive measures for certain individuals thought to pose a risk if not prevented from going about their routine activities. Restricting a particular individual's movements and communications thus becomes a blanket measure to pre-empt any type of displacement[3] from occurring.

7.4 Conclusion

The purpose of this study was twofold, namely to conduct a comparative legal analysis of the control order schemes in the UK and Australia and to compare the underlying mechanisms of control orders to those used in SCP, determining whether pre-emptive laws are in conflict with situational strategies. As such, the first part of the Brief focused on the legal framework and practical implementation of control orders. A statutory analysis sought to identify the provisions giving rise to the pre-emptive issues identified and subsequent critiques; the resultant implementation processes and complications in both the UK and Australia were discussed. Contemporary British control order provisions may not have been introduced as part of emergency legislation, yet their administratively issued civil–criminal hybrid nature enabled them to deviate from well established civil and criminal procedure doctrines, allowing secret evidence to be presented to the judge without a suspect ever being made aware of the accusations against him or her. In an apparent effort to rectify this shortcoming, the UK introduced so-called Special Advocates to view sensitive information on their clients' behalf and represent them. However, as soon as the Special Advocate has consulted the information, any further contact between the two parties was prohibited; making the appointment of Special Advocates appear somewhat quixotic. The Australian system, although restricted by national security considerations, appears to have operated in a more transparent fashion. However, control orders rely heavily on intelligence material in support of the executive decision. Intelligence material does not conform to the more rigorous standards of evidence in court, as the British Home Office established to its detriment when faced with the option of disclosing further, previously closed evidence or having to revoke several control orders. Indeed, the British control order regime was challenged more extensively than its Australian counterpart, likely a by-product of its increased application, as well as the more restrictive obligations, which ultimately lead to its abolition in 2011. That being said, the replacement Terrorism Prevention and Investigation Measures (TPIMs) essentially retained many of the controversial elements of its predecessor, including curfews and restrictions on movement and association, subsequently incurring its own legal challenges. In essence, the underlying mechanisms relied upon to reduce opportunities to offend remain firmly in place.

As a result of their common aim to reduce opportunities to offend, the second part of the Brief drew a number of parallels between the mechanisms by which

[3] i.e. temporal, spatial, target, tactical or offence.

control order restrictions aim to prevent terrorist acts, and the mechanisms through which SCP aims to prevent crime. In essence, control order restrictions can be described as legislated versions of SCP mechanisms. According to Clarke and Newman (2006), changes in legislation and judicial amendments are strategies able to work in conjunction with opportunity reducing techniques. However, control order schemes demonstrate that legislation can be used to directly apply opportunity-reducing strategies. As such, these pre-emptive laws are not in conflict with SCP strategies, and in fact, many of the mechanisms underlying control orders rely on the same approaches of increasing risk and effort associated with offending, removing excuses and reducing provocations for doing so, and attempting to prevent the potential offender from finding suitable targets in the absence of crime controllers. Applied during the pre-crime phase, control order strategies are capable of disrupting criminal lifestyles, the preparation of criminal acts, and groups and networks, thus maximising preventative opportunities.

Given the growing evidence around the effectiveness of SCP interventions, it would appear logical to conclude that control order restrictions prevent the controlee from engaging in terrorist acts. However, a key difference between these two approaches provides cause for concern. Traditionally, SCP methods are targeted at preventing a particular crime type at a particular location by *any* individual motivated to offend. Conversely, whilst the control order's underlying mechanisms may indeed prevent potential suspects from exploiting opportunities to offend, applying these controversial measures selectively against particular individuals merely suspected of terrorist involvement raises important ethical questions. Justified as responding to exceptional risks posed by individuals subject to these orders, in scenarios that focus on the outcomes of particular actions rather than the intentions of would-be offenders, predictions of grave consequence are likely to outweigh all other considerations. Consequently, formalising severely restrictive opportunity-reducing mechanisms in legislation is highly problematic. Measuring prevention, such as accurately estimating the number of crimes prevented by SCP, is fraught with error. Doing so for control orders, however, is considerably more problematic given that both terrorist acts and control orders are such rare events. SCP interventions are generally accepted by society since they do not discriminate and are not coercive. With control orders, on the other hand, it is difficult to assess whether the restrictions on liberty, breaches of due process and fundamental rights and freedoms can ever be justified given our inability to assess their effectiveness with any sort of rigour.

The debate about how to strike the right balance between preventing terrorism and controlling individual suspects is ongoing, and a solution satisfying both parties is unlikely any time soon. Investment in traditional environmentally focused SCP/SPT measures are certainly cable of preventing opportunities to attack at selected vulnerable infrastructure sites. However, as recent events in Boston and Woolwich have highlighted, certain locations or events are more difficult to protect. That being said, using a legal approach to control individuals on the basis of (sensitive) intelligence information alone has proven highly problematic and controversial. As well as reducing opportunities to offend, it is important to remember that the restrictions and obligations contained within control orders (and TPIMs) inherently prevent the police and security services from gathering the very information to be used in subsequent prosecutions. Given this paradox, it appears clear that the traditionally reactive legal route is not suitable for use during the pre-emptive phase. Dealing with such unknowns not only raises several legal issues, but ultimately brings the criminal justice system into disrepute. In conclusion, there needs to be greater emphasis on gathering evidence on those terrorism suspects who currently pose a sufficiently great risk to warrant the imposition of pre-trial coercive measures.

References

Aradau, C., & van Munster, R. (2009). Exceptionalism and the 'War on Terror'. *British Journal of Criminology, 49*, 686–701.

Clare, J., & Morgan, F. (2009). Exploring parallels between situational prevention and non-criminological theories for reducing terrorist risk. In J. D. Freilich & G. R. Newman (Eds.), *Reducing terrorism through situational crime prevention* (Vol. 25, pp. 207–227). Monsey: Criminal Justice Press.

Clarke, R. V. (2008). Situational crime prevention. In R. Wortley & L. Mazerolle (Eds.), *Environmental criminology and crime analysis*. London: Routledge.

Clarke, R. V., & Newman, G. R. (2006). *Outsmarting the terrorists*. Westport: Praeger Security International.

Emerton, P. (2007). Australia's terrorism offences—A case against. In A. Lynch, E. MacDonald, & G. Williams (Eds.), *Law and liberty in the war on terror*. Sydney: Federation Press.

Ericson, R. V. (2007). *Crime in an insecure world*. Cambridge: Polity Press.

Felson, M. (1995). Those who discourage crime. In J. E. Eck & D. Weisburd (Eds.), *Crime and place: Crime prevention studies* (Vol. 4, pp. 53–66). Monsey: Ciminal Justice Press.

Gani, M. (2008). How does it end? Reflections on completed prosecutions under Australia's anti-terrorism legislation. In M. Gani & P. Mathew (Eds.), *Fresh perspectives on the war on terror*. Canberra: ANU E Press.

Goldsmith, A. (2008). The governance of terror: Precautionary logic and counterterrorist law reform after September 11. *Law & Policy, 30*(2), 141–167.

Lord Carlile of Berriew QC. (2007). *The Definition of Terrorism: A Report by Lord Carlile of Berriew Q.C., Independent Reviewer of Terrorism Legislation*. London.

Lynch, A. (2006). Legislating with urgency—the enactment of the anti-terrorism act [no 1] 2005. *Melbourne University Law Review, 30*(3), 747–781.

Lynch, A. (2007). Achieving security, respecting rights and maintaining the rule of law. In A. Lynch, E. MacDonald, & G. Williams (Eds.), *Law and liberty in the war on terror*. Sydney: Federation Press.

Lynch, A., & McGarrity, N. (2008). Australia's Counter-terrorism laws: How neutral laws create fear and anxiety in muslim communities. *Alternative Law Journal, 33*(4), 225–228.

Lynch, A., & Williams, G. (2006). *What price security? Taking stock of australia's anti-terror laws*. Sydney: University of New South Wales Press Ltd.

Manningham-Buller, E. (2005). The International Terrorist Threat and the Dilemmas in Countering It. *Speech By The Director General Of The Security Service, Dame Eliza Manningham-Buller, At The Ridderzaal, Binnenhof, The Hague, Netherlands, 1 September 2005*., from https://www.mi5.gov.uk/output/director-generals-speech-to-the-aivd-2005.html.

Roach, K. (2010). The eroding distinction between intelligence and evidence in terrorism investigations. In N. McGarrity, A. Lynch, & G. Williams (Eds.), *Counter-terrorism and beyond: The culture of law and justice after 9/11*. London: Routledge.

Security Council Resolution 1566, S/RES/1566 (2004), United Nations (2004).

Security Legislation Review Committee. (2006). *Report of the security legislation review committee*. Canberra: Commonwealth of Australia.

Sunstein, C. R. (2005). *Laws of fear: Beyond the precautionary principle*. Cambridge: Cambridge University Press.

Walker, C. (2007). The United Kingdom's anti-terrorism laws: Lessons for Australia. In A. Lynch, E. MacDonald, & G. Williams (Eds.), *Law and liberty in the war on terror*. Sydney: Federation Press.

Zedner, L. (2006). Neither safe nor sound? The perils and possibilities of risk. *Canadian Journal of Criminology and Criminal Justice, 48*(3), 423–434.

Zedner, L. (2007). Preventive justice or pre-punishment? The case of control orders. *Current Legal Problems, 60*(1), 174–203. doi:10.1093/clp/60.1.174.

Zedner, L. (2009). Fixing the future? The pre-emptive turn in criminal justice. In B. McSherry, A. Norrie, & S. Bronitt (Eds.), *Regulating deviance: The redirection of criminalisation and the futures of criminal law*. Oxford: Hart Publishing.

MIX
Papier aus verantwortungsvollen Quellen
Paper from responsible sources
FSC® C105338

If you have any concerns about our products,
you can contact us on
ProductSafety@springernature.com

In case Publisher is established outside the EU,
the EU authorized representative is:
Springer Nature Customer Service Center GmbH
Europaplatz 3, 69115 Heidelberg, Germany

Printed by Libri Plureos GmbH
in Hamburg, Germany